THE LETTERS OF
PIERRE ELLIOTT TRUDEAU
AND MARSHALL MCLUHAN

Been Hoping We Might Meet Again

ELAINE KAHN

NOVALIS

Cover design: Martin Gould
Cover photograph: Getty Images
Layout: Audrey Wells

Published by Novalis

Publishing Office
1 Eglinton Avenue East, Suite 800
Toronto, Ontario, Canada
M4P 3A1

Head Office
4475 Frontenac Street
Montréal, Québec, Canada
H2H 2S2

www.novalis.ca

Library and Archives Canada Cataloguing in Publication

Been hoping we might meet again : the letters of Pierre Elliott Trudeau and Marshall McLuhan / Elaine Kahn, editor.
ISBN 978-2-89688-588-6 (softcover)

1. Trudeau, Pierre Elliott, 1919-2000--Correspondence. 2. McLuhan, Marshall, 1911-1980--Correspondence. 3. Prime ministers--Canada--Correspondence. 4. Authors, Canadian (English)--20th century--Correspondence. 5. Mass media specialists--Canada--Correspondence. 6. Catholics--Canada--Correspondence. I. Kahn, Elaine, 1953-, editor

FC626.T7A4 2019 971.064'6092 C2018-905044-6

Printed in Canada.

We acknowledge the support of the Government of Canada.

5 4 3 2 1 23 22 21 20 19

For Larry

sine quo non

Contents

Foreword

Congenial Minds, *Ante Litteram*

Let's try for a moment to imagine the world we would be living in today if two Canadian 20th-century intellectual giants, Pierre Trudeau and Marshall McLuhan, had never existed. The great changes that have affected contemporary society in the last half-century would probably still have occurred. By virtue of its geopolitical position, Canada would still have become the civil rights–based multicultural country it is today. The world would still be a large, hyper-connected village. The medium would have trumped the message, *notwithstanding*. But something would have been missing.

This unique collection of letters has the merit of bringing to light some of those missing elements: above all, a vision. Both Trudeau and McLuhan let themselves be inspired by a visionary instinct in search of the *spirit of the times*. As the world became a global theatre, these two modern visionaries shared the same stage with the intent to evoke and provoke, animate and irritate, challenging the intelligentsia of the time, surrounded by the destiny of receiving praise and criticism in equal measure. Yet the visionary instinct, as we know, is nourished by passion – always to be put after reason! That same controversial passion was capable of generating the wave of *Trudeaumania* or infecting hordes of proselytes with *mcluhanite*, inside and outside Canada.

Indeed, this is the fate of those pop icons whom the 20th century has elevated to modern myths. In the case of Trudeau and McLuhan, two authentic Canadian brands, their impact has also taken on, and not by chance, linguistic nuances – Trudeauism and McLuhanism have become part of the national thesaurus. In this regard, it must be said that a further merit of this volume lies in restoring a portrait of both the fine lawyer and the unconventional professor free from the usual clichés: that is, capable of going beyond those stereotypes through which people have pretended to understand them.

If Trudeau and McLuhan had never existed, we would not have been able to enjoy the astonishing linguistic acrobatics with which both have been able to embellish themselves. The letters collected here show a voracious and common passion, a genuine fascination with language. In fact, they both spoke to the country, not only releasing new ideas, but also coining a new vocabulary – sometimes with macho traits: "Just watch me!" (Trudeau) or, as a joker, "You don't like my ideas? I have others!" (McLuhan). Trudeau, whom McLuhan would call a made-for-TV politician, had to exercise the power of communication at an age when reality was built to perfection – a phenomenon that McLuhan would describe through one of his brilliant oxymorons, a "genuine fake" (March 26, 1974). Our oral alchemists knew that language is not so much a tool for expressing thought, but the very condition for thinking – it not only gives form to thought, but transforms it. And so it is that the letters reveal a playful exchange of one-line jokes *à la* McLuhan, such as "As Zeus said to Narcissus: 'Watch yourself!'" as well as quotations, paraphrases and sparks of genius hidden between the folds of the words.

Now let's try to make a further imaginative effort. What would have happened if those letters had not been delivered? Or if Trudeau and McLuhan had never met?

Again, they would both have gone their respective ways – Trudeau, a resolute leader, worn out by 16 long years in power; McLuhan, a media prophet, crushed by that timid giant the TV, which he himself had helped people to understand. If the two had never met, perhaps today we would have a slightly different idea of Canada, or maybe Canada itself would be different. Against the backdrop of the intellectual marriage described in these letters are the themes and issues that have marked the events of modern Canada. Trudeau was not one of the many curious people who appeared in the court of McLuhan. The construction of a vision was at stake. In his summer 1975 letters, McLuhan portrays Canada as a world Utopia, "the only country in the world without an identity," because "on the frontier everybody is a nobody" – an analysis, once again played out through words, that would undoubtedly have intrigued any prime minister, and in fact reveals the reasons for a deep affinity that reverberates in those letters.

Elaine Kahn's painstaking work, digging through hundreds of documents at Library and Archives Canada over eight years, gives us a unique account of the spiritual afflatus that distinguishes the two intellectuals, not shown in public. The letters disclose a sort of religious intimacy, revealed in crescendo as the relationship between the two becomes closer and more convivial. Reading these letters today is a bit like looking through the keyhole into the depths of two minds, two men of letters, two men of faith, resonating with each other.

This precious correspondence, enriched by the useful commentaries that guide the understanding of the context and add pleasant details, gives us a very generous portrait of the two masquerade celebrities. Time, as we know, is gentlemanly and leads us to apply a sort of *notwithstanding clause* to the judgment that the world has *a posteriori* reserved for these two charismatic, telegenic and unpredictable representatives of an entire generation. Their vibrant legacy is still present; their thought, always one step ahead, we found on the road to the future. It is enlightening to read the laconic comment made by Trudeau's colleague J.M. Davey about McLuhan: "I believe that we can get the greatest value from the horizons that he can open to our thinking rather than illumination of the path immediately ahead" (December 13, 1968). Trudeau and McLuhan have lived as men of the future, which does not necessarily mean knowing how to predict the future, but rather making it happen, ahead of the times of history. "I am strongly convinced that ... the 'global village' will gradually take shape as a true city, i.e. a place worth living for all mankind," writes Trudeau on March 17, 1975.

That city is the ideal locus of creative virtue: namely, the ability to create the future with intellect, fantasy and imagination. After all, the global theatre invites us to live a creative life, providing us with the interface to manifest a creativity that makes life worthy of being fully lived: that is, to facilitate a creative outlet, a vision that shapes the future, *ante litteram.*

Paolo Granata, Assistant Professor in Book and Media Studies,
St. Michael's College in the University of Toronto

A Canadian Interval in the Global Village

The identity process of which you speak so often is one that cannot be ignored by government. I am very much aware of the sometimes search and sometimes struggle for new images in which many communities of our society are engaging. What I lack is an intuitive process to forecast for me the likeliest form of a satisfactory nature which these new images will assume. Can you help me?

Pierre Elliott Trudeau to Marshall McLuhan,
November 25, 1968

This is a story of two Canadian men, Marshall McLuhan and Pierre Elliott Trudeau, learning about and shaping their nation and the global village as public intellectuals in the late 20th century. They had separate paths, but they had intersections, including a growing personal relationship lasting a dozen years, from McLuhan's first letter to Trudeau in April 1968 to McLuhan's death in December 1980. Trudeau, Canada's first international political star, was on the rise during this period; McLuhan, global prophet of media ecology, was already becoming yesterday's news. Their correspondence, annotated, never before studied as a discrete subject or published in its entirety, is the heart of this cultural history.

The letter quoted above is the only time I've read of Trudeau asking so bluntly for help. It was uncharacteristic for Trudeau to show such vulnerability, according to at least one critic who, comparing Trudeau with his predecessor, Lester "Mike" Pearson, wrote:

> Mike always made you feel you were needed even if this was far from the case. Pierre makes you feel he doesn't give a shit even though he may need you badly. He just can't bring himself to say "Help me," though if the phrase passed his lips a hundred people would rush to his aid.[1]

In the McLuhan-Trudeau relationship, the help did flow mainly from the professor to the perpetual student.

Their correspondence is housed at Library and Archives Canada (LAC) in Ottawa; some of the letters have appeared in bits in books written about them. In 1987, Oxford University Press published a fascinating selection of McLuhan's letters; no published collection of Trudeau's letters exists. The two men were at the forefront of discussions about critical issues of globalization, especially the political uses of media, at a time when globalization was not yet a recognized keyword in the literature. All this is reflected in the letters, as well as their shared Catholicism. The current Canadian prime minister, Justin Trudeau, was born during the period covered by the correspondence.

Rulers and politicians have always had advisors helping them communicate with others, but the Trudeau-McLuhan relationship was the first time a politician was getting advice that so presciently took into account the globalizing, digitalizing world.

They inspired me. They understood, as I have always understood, that globalism goes far beyond economics, that corporations may run the world but individual human beings live it, often cooperatively, and that the most exciting, if often volatile, points in that global village are in the resonating intervals.

The letters are the second chapter of this book, the intersection between this slice of their stories and fragments of mine, grappling with globalization, multiculturalism, borders. I do recognize the surface

---

1 Christina McCall, *My Life as a Dame: The Personal and the Political in the Writings of Christina McCall.* Edited by Stephen Clarkson. Toronto: House of Anansi, 2008, 301.

strangeness of a Jewish feminist woman searching for resonances with two dead white Catholic men.

The relationship between these two intellects was warm and nuanced. Trudeau "spoke of McLuhan with great reverence" and, for McLuhan, Trudeau was "an image of the age, a phenomenon of media, a rare combination of training, practice, intuition, vision; a figure of undoubted fascination, a charismatic who manifested the Canadian dualities and ambiguities."[2] Both were experts at media manipulation and recognized that in the other. McLuhan was teaching the world and Trudeau about the global village at the same time as Trudeau was helping Canada find its place and meanings in it. Even a cursory glance at the news today shows how much their work is still relevant and needs to be built upon.

Although almost a decade younger than McLuhan, Trudeau becomes the senior figure in the story, not only because he lived longer and remained involved with global affairs after his time in office, but because his struggles for a united Canada and his considerations of nationalism and Quebec have intriguing parallels in the constant struggles of a globalizing world (and a still periodically restless Quebec). He knew from experience that

> the distinction often drawn by nationalists between "good" nationalism (mine) and "bad" nationalism (yours) did not stand up to serious analysis. Nationalism in all its manifestations stood for ethnic homogeneity and cultural conformity. Modern, progressive societies were nourished by ethnic plurality and cultural hybridity.[3]

Each of them has been called a "citizen of the world" – the term is used of McLuhan in the introduction to the collection of his letters and of Trudeau, quoting him as a youth, as the title of the first book of the two-volume biography by John English. But I think Trudeau was the more thoughtfully engaged global citizen, politically and culturally. By all accounts, including his own, McLuhan was a reluctant inhabitant

2 Private email to me from B.W. Powe, February 9, 2017.

3 Ramsay Cook, *The Teeth of Time: Remembering Pierre Elliott Trudeau*. Montreal: McGill-Queen's University Press, 2006, 32.

of the 20th century, almost never watching the very medium, television, that he explained so well (neither did Trudeau) and viewing the global village as a place of retribalization and terror. He wrote, "Globes make my head spin. By the time I locate the place, they've changed the boundaries."[4]

The McLuhan archive in Ottawa contains about 800,000 pieces of paper, 100,000 pages of that being letters. Trudeau was instrumental in keeping the archive in Canada.[5] Ideas are often reused, as is usually true of anyone's correspondence and as is true of McLuhan's work in general. McLuhan kept extensive clippings files; I've noted some wonderful juxtapositions which I'm sure were not lost on him, given his own writings on the strange interfaces of stories on any given page of a newspaper. His files contain a political cartoon of Trudeau as a playful, and slightly creepy, Pied Piper, from the April 8, 1968, edition of the *Toronto Telegram*; on the back of the cartoon is a photo of Coretta King and her children by the side of her husband's coffin. One must pay attention to the whole picture.

McLuhan wrote that the medium is the message.[6] Something that is medium is somewhere in the middle, mediating. That median, that interface, that gap where something new can be created or understood, where understanding of the other becomes a possibility, where education happens, enthralls me. McLuhan later changed his message to "the medium is the massage," the title of his 1967 book with Quentin Fiore. Like so much of his work, he was partly serious here and partly punning and could almost never be pinned down to one meaning for anything, which contributed greatly to people not taking him seriously. I have massaged the letters to release their messages, but my passion for them is grounded in the fact that they exist at all. Other readers will find their own meanings and new questions resonating in the juxtapositions.

---

4 Marshall McLuhan and Quentin Fiore, *War and Peace in the Global Village*. New York: McGraw-Hill, 1968, frontispiece.

5 Matie Molinaro, Corinne McLuhan and William Toye, eds., *Letters of Marshall McLuhan*. Toronto: Oxford University Press, 1987, viii, for the size of the archives. Trudeau's role is cited by a number of sources.

6 Marshall McLuhan, *Understanding Media: The Extensions of Man*. New York: Signet, 1964, 23.

Trudeau, a constitutional lawyer and enthusiastic global traveller,[7] enticed by politics and discomfited by the very media realities he learned to master, was prime minister of Canada almost continuously from 1968 to 1984. University of Toronto professor Marshall McLuhan gave us "global village" and gave the new field of media ecology its theoretical grounding, but he extolled neither the citizens of that village nor the new media shaping them. By 1968, new media were already profoundly shaping one of Trudeau's core constituencies, even if one largely too young to vote for him: my generation. Especially in this year of the centenary of Trudeau's birth, attention must be paid to the intersecting of these two extraordinary men.

I have been fascinated by Trudeau and McLuhan since high school. Others have written about their lives, the influences on them, and their ideas. I am the first to specifically puzzle out in some detail the interaction between them, especially on topics such as Canada's place in the world, multiculturalism and the management of media. The Trudeau-McLuhan correspondence has been background music in some studies, not looked at as the resonant creative interval it is. "The 'missing link' created far more interest than all the chains and explanations of being."[8]

I have thought about how they were global citizens, how they thought of Canada as part of a global village, how Quebec nationalism fit into that picture. Were their discussions of foreign policy ever any more substantial than McLuhan volunteering his opinions of world leaders? In his July 6, 1973, letter to Trudeau, for example, he included an unpublished piece about Richard Nixon[9] ("Mr. Nixon and the Dropout Strategy"), and a February 24, 1977, letter discussed Jimmy Carter.[10]

The more important question is this: In what ways did McLuhan give Trudeau the help he was asked to give?

The two friends were influential figures at a particular time in Canadian history, when the global village was in the early stages of

---

7 According to his wife, however, "The Canadians, I soon found, don't really like their prime minister traveling despite the fact that internationally Pierre has put Canada on the map." Margaret Trudeau, *Beyond Reason*. New York: Paddington Press, 1979, 154.

8 Marshall McLuhan, *Culture is Our Business*. New York: McGraw-Hill, 1970, 114.

9 President of the United States from 1969 to 1974.

10 President of the United States from 1977 to 1981.

becoming something more than alternate wording for "multinational corporation," and Canada was figuring out how to become a multicultural country with its own constitution, while still threatened by Quebec separatism. As Robertson Davies wrote, "The Canadians knew themselves to be strangers in their own land, without being at home anywhere else."[11] Canada is often a middle land, an interface; the Upper Canada Preserved medal, struck to honour patriots of the War of 1812, depicts a Canadian beaver being protected by a British lion against an American eagle.[12] More recently, commenting on both the then-pending 2016 US presidential election and the UK vote on whether to remain part of the European Union, one journalist wrote that "in between the two riled colossuses of the English world, there is genteel Canada, probably striking some kind of yoga pose, possibly about to be overrun by fleeing Brits and Yanks."[13]

It's been more than 40 years since one scholar noted that "The major difference between Canadians and Americans on the subject of their relationship is in the intensity of their perceptions. There is bound to be a conflict between a people who regard their relationship as critical and those who have scarcely noticed the other country."[14]

This is a story of history, informed by current events. This is also a story of borders, although the word itself never appears in the correspondence. I am intolerant of borders; in my own story, I have immigrants and refugees and others not lucky enough to find refuge. Borders can be so harsh, used not only to delineate political jurisdictions but also to isolate and manipulate ethnicities, including, today, through the sale of citizenship and passports in an enormous perversion of what is meant by both nationality and globalization. "It is easy to imagine a scenario in which large groups of displaced people or minorities in a country that would sooner see them gone – Myanmar's Rohingya population, for example – are forced to take a foreign nationality under duress and are then sent away," says a writer who tracks this injustice

11 Robertson Davies, *World of Wonders*. Markham: Penguin Books Canada, 1975, 260.

12 http://www.napoleon-series.org/military/Warof1812/2007/Issue6/c_benn.html

13 http://www.cbc.ca/news/politics/wherry-trudeau-brexit-trump-1.3651482

14 John W. Holmes, "Impact of Domestic Political Factors on Canadian-American Relations: Canada." *International Organization* 28:4 (1974): 611–635, at 611.

closely.[15] "For all the talk of an interconnected, 'flat' world, being born with a bad passport is still a great misfortune… [the] pitch to [wealthy] people is this: In the modern world, borders are still very much erect – but they can be flattened, for a price."[16]

This is a story, too, of the interpretations generated when borders meet, creating friction, or when they approach each other and meaning is created in the space, the interval, holding them with some kind of creative force. "All boundaries are areas of maximal abrasion and change," McLuhan wrote. "The interval or gap constitutes the resonant or musical bond in the material universe. This is where the action is."[17] There can also be abrasion between generations, and Trudeau needed to remain attractive to young people. McLuhan, approaching him with ways he might engage on television with high school and university students, wrote:

> They are not looking for "feed-back" but "feed-forward." It would be inevitable that as soon as they began to discuss their problems there would begin a resonance with many problems of your own. It would be perfectly natural for you to illustrate and to discuss their problems while briefing them on yours. They in turn could comment on yours, setting up a natural interface between areas of community life on one hand, and government on the other. Such an encounter via TV has never occurred before.[18]

It is not even certain how and where the two men met or first became aware of each other. One biographer writes that McLuhan first noticed Trudeau in the 1950s.[19] The Trudeau archives has a photocopy from the November 21, 1965, *New York World Journal Tribune* of Tom Wolfe's "What if He is Right," a profile of McLuhan later republished in Wolfe's 1968 *The Pump House Gang*. A handwritten notation in a July 3, 1968,

15 Atossa Araxia Abrahamian, "When citizenship is for sale." *The New York Times*, January 7, 2018.

16 Atossa Araxia Abrahamian, *The Cosmopolites: The Coming of the Global Citizen*. New York: Columbia Global Reports, 2015, 73.

17 Marshall McLuhan and Barrington Nevitt, *Take Today: The Executive as Dropout*. New York: Harcourt Brace Jovanovich, 1972, 3.

18 McLuhan to Trudeau, October 17, 1968.

19 Nino Ricci, *Pierre Elliott Trudeau*. Toronto: Penguin Group, 2009, 100.

letter from Trudeau to McLuhan refers to a brief encounter in June 1964 in Charlottetown. McLuhan is not mentioned in Trudeau's memoirs, but neither are others known to be friends, such as Max and Monique Nemni, who have published two volumes of his intellectual biography.

According to another writer,

> Trudeau's capers, from the girls he kissed to the clothes he wore, were always calculated for effect. He was always careful of the reporters to whom he gave interviews. One of the first experts he consulted when he ran for the leadership was communication specialist Marshall McLuhan.[20]

This suggests the initial outreach came from Trudeau, or possibly from intermediary James Davey, the British-born physicist who was a member of Trudeau's inner circle of advisors, but the correspondence suggests otherwise.

McLuhan wrote his first letter to Trudeau during the year he was teaching at Fordham University in New York and living in Bronxville, next door to television icon Jack Paar, host of the *Tonight* show. In that letter, McLuhan alludes to a number of issues important to him that will recur in the correspondence – it is almost as if the rest of the letters unpack the first. Those issues include both "media" and various media, Canadian identity, post-Fordism (though he doesn't use that term), religion, Canada–US relations and the use of image in politics.

Their relationship was sparked shortly after the assassination of Martin Luther King, Jr., and took off between then and the assassination of Robert Kennedy, a two-month period coinciding almost exactly with Trudeau's election to the leadership of the Liberal party and then the prime ministership. Students were openly protesting all over the Western world and the Vietnam War was escalating. At the same time, the use of media to best advantage became a boom industry – a less positive take would note that it had been only a few years since Daniel Boorstin coined and demonstrated the insidious uses of the "pseudo-event,"[21] insights which have skyrocketed in value in the years since.

20 Walter Stewart, *Shrug: Trudeau in Power*. Toronto: New Press, 1971, 7.

21 Daniel J. Boorstin, *The Image: A Guide to Pseudo-events in America*. New York: Vintage Books, 1992, 7.

Canada, so proud of the global impression it had made by marking its centennial with the 1967 World's Fair, Expo '67, began to legislate in favour of multiculturalism. This was an attempt to become more accommodating to the "other" than had resulted from the previous concept of a Canadian mosaic. The Royal Commission on Bilingualism and Biculturalism had already been working since 1963 to understand and more widely implement Canada's basic cultural dualism. The even more expansive idea of mosaic had been infiltrating the public consciousness for a decade, culminating in 1965 with the publication of sociologist John Porter's *The Vertical Mosaic* and providing a new model to contrast with the US melting pot. In his October 17, 1968, letter to Trudeau, McLuhan referred to student power groups in high schools and colleges as "a Canadian mosaic." But, in a mosaic, the pieces don't touch.

For many Canadians of that generation, including me, the centennial and some years on either side of it were a time not only of celebration and pride, but also of a belief, or maybe a willed belief, that Canada's time had come, that she would finally land a big role on the big world stage. Always a place that had defined itself, even before it was a country, in relation to the United States, usually in some kind of dysfunctional sibling rivalry, Canada was ready to lead – or at least most of the country, the parts still known as English Canada, believed itself ready. Quebec had (and often through not-so-benign neglect was allowed to have) its own concerns. Sometimes those concerns overlapped, other times there was friction, sometimes the meeting point resonated.

In its initial phases, Canadian multiculturalism on a practical level was largely a matter of local festivals and celebrations at which people sampled foods from various ethnic groups or watched folk dancers in ethnic costumes. Within a couple of decades, it had become a more sophisticated tapestry of understanding and visibility which by now has reshaped the country. Similarly, although "global village" is today part of our vocabulary (some might even call it a cliché), it was "novel and puzzling" when McLuhan first used it.[22]

22 Léon Surette, referring to the use of the term in McLuhan's 1961 seminar class [McLuhan100 Then Now Next: International Conference, Toronto, ON, November 7-10, 2011].

Trudeau may not have taken a lot of ideas from McLuhan – it can be argued more than one way – but it was important to Trudeau to be exposed to them and certainly it was important to McLuhan to pass them along. He gave his books to the prime minister and Trudeau was not merely being polite when he thanked McLuhan for doing so. The prime minister looked forward to reading them; he cherished intellectual stimulation. "Blessed with an exceptional memory, he read omnivorously and with a ferocious, head-down tenacity."[23] Listening to others, and questioning them, was apparently typical of Trudeau, a characteristic I think did not come through to the general public.[24] Even before his contact with McLuhan, he was aware of the technological and scientific revolution taking place, and he recognized that any nation which did not join in would become a new kind of "banana republic."[25]

The public inclusion of McLuhan's work in Trudeau's was also likely influenced by which advisors Trudeau had at any given time. His first cohort included several intellectuals, and a number of his speeches early in his first term included references to McLuhan or his work.

In an April 1969 magazine interview, for example, the prime minister spoke in perfect McLuhanese of the younger generation's penchant for "dropping out" and cited directly McLuhan's idea about the sophistication of that generation in comparison with his own:

> Marshall McLuhan has helped us all to realize a lot of things in this area; how a child of three or four learns things on television which we learned when we were only 18 or 19. I'm not thinking necessarily of events, I'm thinking of images. They see pictures of fighting and dying. They are aware of wars abroad and great events happening everywhere in the world.[26]

23 Richard Gwyn, *The Northern Magus: Pierre Trudeau and Canadians*. Toronto: McClelland & Stewart, 1980, 32.

24 According to Patrick Gossage, one of Trudeau's press secretaries, "There are lots of books by Trudeau cabinet ministers, and they were all just amazed at how he ran cabinet meetings and got the best out of everybody and listened – how decisions were made as a team rather than one man imposing his will." http://www.cbc.ca/news/politics/now-that-justin-trudeau-is-going-to-be-pm-will-he-channel-his-dad-1.3283734

25 Gwyn, *Northern Magus*, 48.

26 Pierre Elliott Trudeau, *Conversation with Canadians*. Toronto: University of Toronto Press, 1972, 11.

Canada's ability to make and keep the peace between warring factions still loomed high in the public imagination, because it hadn't been too long since Lester Pearson had won the 1957 Nobel Peace Prize – and global recognition – for his work on the Suez crisis. During Canada's year of centennial glory, Pearson was prime minister; his justice minister, Trudeau, had already introduced legislation to decriminalize homosexuality.

The Trudeau–McLuhan story is enriched by bringing their letters together, because of the meanings that grow when disparate ideas are brought into creative friction at their point of meeting – one interpretation of McLuhan's "resonant interval."[27] McLuhan advised Trudeau on whatever struck his fancy, including media, politics and religion. "My forte is structural analysis of new problems and environments that, unawares to us, re-program our sensory lives," he wrote the prime minister. (December 2, 1968) "In effect, I am saying that it is now possible to by-pass what used to be called 'fate' by anticipating the effects of new man-made environments."

McLuhan could be almost obsequious. Other times, he felt free to complain, occasionally in a passive-aggressive way. His July 30, 1975, letter to Trudeau mixed both tendencies with his ongoing role as mentor: he apologized for taking up the prime minister's time, taught about individualism and capital punishment, and, before referring to some attached jokes, noted that "One of the strange things I have discovered about my own work is that Westerners in general resent having the effects of any technology brought to their attention... The person who is blamed for this, is the person who points it out to them."

McLuhan was not shy with Trudeau, chiding the new prime minister early on (October 17, 1968) for taking time off in the months after he was first elected. "The time is long overdue for you to be back in circulation," he wrote, "and to be in the Canadian living room as a 'gap-bridger,' the unifying image of our society that you became during the election." And sometimes he didn't take into account the brilliance of

27 "To this day, the French term *McLuhanisme* describes the junction of discrepant worlds that can mingle and intersect, bringing illumination to one another." Eric McLuhan and Frank Zingrone, eds., *Essential McLuhan*. Toronto: House of Anansi, 1995, 270.

his student. Surely Trudeau did not need McLuhan to decode his mixed ancestry for him, as when he pointed out, "The fur-traders, who are mostly Scots, intermarried with the French very freely." (May 29, 1969)

Just the glow of the prime minister's celebrity was a draw for the always star-struck professor. McLuhan was not a sophisticate in the same way as the prime minister and not as interested in international affairs, although he wanted very much to be an advisor to world leaders even if the bulk of that advice was a restating of material published years earlier. During the height of his popularity in the 1960s, McLuhan was sought out by politicians and business leaders globally, but I'm not convinced he ever internalized aspects of the wider world in the same way as Trudeau, who emerged from his global travels "like Ulysses, as part of all he'd met. Few modern statesmen have come to office knowing so much about the world. Trudeau hadn't just been nearly everywhere; he understood how societies worked."[28]

The global village was McLuhan's plaything and he did often travel to spread his message (for example, to international conferences such as the annual Delos symposium off the coast of Athens and, at least once, as he told Trudeau on May 29, 1969, to the annual Bilderberg conference), but his wife, Corinne, and the University of Toronto were his home. In the main, all his work was applicable globally, rather than being specific to Canada, but it wasn't always understandable. Trudeau wrote clearly which, clearly, McLuhan did not.

As Philip Marchand, one of McLuhan's biographers, wrote of his own observations during a year spent helping organize the McLuhan archives in Ottawa,

> No one who is fond of McLuhan can be happy reading certain letters that he wrote on controversial topics to men who held political or academic power. No matter how close to his heart the issue was – and no matter how urgent and valid his protest – McLuhan often seemed compelled, in these letters, to haul out an involved and barely comprehensible (because McLuhan was too impatient to include

28 Gwyn, *Northern Magus*, 40.

> logical links or otherwise fully to explain himself) discussion of figure versus ground, acoustic versus visual space, North Americans going out to be alone, or some other characteristic theme. One can see the eyes of the recipient rolling upwards at the sight of these paragraphs.[29]

Trudeau's responses to McLuhan were gracious, albeit usually much briefer than the letters to which he was responding. Marchand noted that

> McLuhan rarely used this correspondence to lobby Trudeau on specific issues, which was certainly wise. Rather, in McLuhan's parlance, he tried to draw attention to the hidden "ground" of the "figure" constituted by certain specific issues. Trudeau's replies to McLuhan's letters are both respectful and thoughtful, but obviously those of a man living in a different mental universe.[30]

"Figure" and "ground" are valuable concepts; it's just that they have so completely worked themselves into the contemporary mindset that they lack the power to startle as they might have done when McLuhan was first playing with them. When considering these two men, it's good to look at not only the figures themselves but the ground they came from and were seen against. On the surface, what they had in common was their Canadian citizenship, devotion to their mothers (though McLuhan preferred to keep his at a distance), prankishness, Catholicism (which they approached quite differently), an interest in psychology, a prodigious ability to memorize poetry, a disdain for the mob[31] and great rapport with young people, even if apparently there was quite a difference in their skills as a father. The ease with which they made reference to philosophers, artists and writers without explanation indicates an assumption that there was still some shared basic knowledge among certain educated classes.

29 Philip Marchand, "Some Comments on the McLuhan Papers in the National Archives of Canada." *Canadian Journal of Communications*/Special Issue (1989): 14:4, 67–72 at 68.

30 Marchand, "Some Comments," 69.

31 Gwyn, *Northern Magus*, 117.

The letters contain frequent references to figure and ground. In the 20th century, McLuhan wrote, Canada itself played "the role of hidden *ground* for big powers."[32] In another interpretation,

> 'Figure' was visual, conceptual, the ascribed cause of a thing. 'Ground' was acoustic, perceptual, the perceived effect of a thing. Ground was a medium as McLuhan had always studied a medium – when he had noted the relationship between, say, print and nationalism. It was the environment, it was the source of all real change.[33]

McLuhan connects this to his thoughts about left hemisphere/right hemisphere theories of the brain, increasingly popular at the time, when writing to Trudeau on September 3, 1976:

> For thirty years at least, I have been using the two hemisphere approach under the names of the <u>written</u> and the <u>oral</u>, the <u>visual</u> and the <u>acoustic</u>, the <u>hot</u> and the <u>cool</u>, the <u>medium</u> and the <u>message</u>, <u>figure</u> and <u>ground</u>, and so on. Now it turns out that medicine has been building a great beach-head for this approach with its new understanding of the two hemispheres of the brain.
>
> My work has been a dialogue between the two hemispheres in which the characteristics of the right hemisphere are given so much recognition that I have been unintelligible to the left hemisphere people.

McLuhan saw "medium" not as television, radio and so on, but as the environment or ground for figure.[34]

I try to always keep in mind that, although Trudeau lived long enough to be part of the global personally-wired world, McLuhan, who predicted much of what has come to pass in and from that wired

32 Marshall McLuhan, "Canada: The Borderline Case," in *The Canadian Imagination: Dimensions of a Literary Culture*. Edited by David Staines. Cambridge: Harvard University Press, 1977, 227.

33 Philip Marchand, *Marshall McLuhan: The Medium and Messenger*. Cambridge: The MIT Press, 1998, 260.

34 Eric McLuhan [McLuhan100 Then Now Next: International Conference, Toronto, ON, November 7-10, 2011].

world, did not. They communicated by letters (often dictated),[35] phone and personal visits, a vastly slower pace than would be the case today. McLuhan typed many of his own letters. Trudeau used a fountain pen, usually with blue ink, for the notes he made on the letters I've seen and for his signature. If weeks or months go by between letters, that doesn't guarantee a lack of interest or amity – it could indicate the nonexistence of email.

I've found no evidence that either was computer-literate. They seem to have come no closer than guilt by association: "Almost everyone likens Trudeau's mind to a computer: capacious, inexhaustible, and precise"[36] and McLuhan has been described as "a natural-born interfacer" with a hypertextual mind.[37] They were people of the book. In the decade before McLuhan died, he showed little interest "in exploring the implications of the latest advances – not even that great technological wonder of the seventies, the microchip computer. For him, electronic technology was largely broadcasting – instantaneous, global communications."[38]

With some of their letters – for example, the August 2, 1972, letter from McLuhan to Trudeau – one can feel the indentations of the typewriting on the paper. As I sat transfixed by documents at the archives in Ottawa, I ran my fingers across them over and over. And I too use a fountain pen.

Joseph Philippe Pierre Yves Elliott Trudeau was born in Montreal on October 18, 1919, the middle child and first son of Charles Trudeau and Grace Elliott. He married Margaret Sinclair in 1971 and they had three sons before divorcing in 1984. Trudeau subsequently had a daughter through his relationship with Deborah Coyne. He died on September 28, 2000.

Although the letters don't focus on the domestic life of either man, that aspect does resonate in the background. Trudeau's public life espe-

35 McLuhan seems to have handwritten all his letters until around 1959. Molinaro, Corinne McLuhan and Toye, eds., *Letters*, 253, footnote 1.

36 Gwyn, *Northern Magus*, 50.

37 Derrick de Kerckhove [McLuhan100 Then Now Next: International Conference, Toronto, ON, November 7-10, 2011].

38 Marchand, *Medium and Messenger*, 264.

cially was intertwined with his private one. Trudeau and Margaret set their wedding date while he was already dealing with the 1970 October Crisis, arguably the most controversial period of his lengthy time as prime minister. Trudeau seems to have been a much better father than McLuhan, but his marriage ended badly and publicly. The image of Pierre and Margaret became a media circus that put Canada on the global stage, from their wedding through their marriage through the separation and divorce.

Trudeau's political passions were federalism, which itself is a negotiation of rights and duties across boundaries, civil rights (despite his imposition of the War Measures Act) and the recognition of a wider world beyond Quebec and beyond Canada. His goal of a Canadian Bill of Rights and Constitution was single-minded, once he was dedicated to it; initially, while serving under Pearson, he was against the government taking on the issue.[39] His active Catholicism, which ultimately became liberal, may have also widened his outlook. I believe his worldview, based on a strong social consciousness, became genuinely global, even though those closest to him throughout his life tended to come from the white Canadian establishment into which he was born.

There were regular family vacations to the United States, especially to Old Orchard Beach in Maine, a regular haunt of wealthy Québécois. Hugh MacLennan didn't publish his influential novel *Two Solitudes*, some of which takes place in Old Orchard Beach, until 1945, but, as has been much documented, Trudeau's family was itself an interface of the two solitudes, French and Anglo.[40]

Trudeau, fit and healthy most of his life, was highly competitive, though mainly in activities, such as wilderness canoeing, that pitted individual against individual or against nature. His lifelong passion for experiencing the natural world led him to work on environmental issues, which gave him an involvement in the global commons. McLuhan's environmental interests appear to be more site specific – for example, protesting against Toronto's Spadina Expressway, which would have run

39 Pierre Elliott Trudeau, *Memoirs*. Toronto: McClelland & Stewart, 1993, 228.

40 This is the standard way of defining the solitudes, though those of Scottish descent, like Trudeau, might argue over their inclusion as "Anglo."

through the city and was cancelled, partially built, in 1971, after such protests. Even here there is an interface, as one of McLuhan's fellow protesters was urban planning activist Jane Jacobs, a friend of Trudeau's.[41] At times, Trudeau spoke of the environment as something that must be confronted by countries working together in the global village.[42]

Trudeau's father died suddenly of a heart attack when Trudeau was young, leaving him as man of the house. His childhood home, with his mother, was his base until he became prime minister; through his 20s, he attended daily Mass with Grace, and throughout his life he rarely missed Sunday Mass.[43] Trudeau was given a parochial, Catholic, French Quebec–centred education, from his years at the conservative Jesuit Collège Jean-de-Brébeuf through law school at the Université de Montréal. That education reflected the narrowness and prejudices of his time and class, including anti-Semitism, and he absorbed and promulgated all of it with no apparent trouble. His further education outside Canada, starting with his graduate studies in economics at Harvard, began to broaden him, as did his travels. At the London School of Economics, for example, Trudeau came under the influence of Harold Laski, who was a Jew.

> In all likelihood, the notion of multiculturalism Trudeau later came to espouse in Canada actually had its roots in these first real experiences outside the country. The Montreal of his childhood was hardly monocultural, yet he had lived it as such, where everyone who was other – the English, the immigrants, the Jews – was the enemy. Now the boundaries between "us" and "them" were dissolving; it was in this sense that he truly became a "citizen of the world."[44]

Trudeau was forever an engaged Catholic, both in practice and in his intellectual grappling, but his approach to his religion changed from

41 McCall, *My Life as a Dame,* 116.

42 According to Jacobs, Canadian identity was a matter of good common sense that made Canadians respond "to what Marshall McLuhan calls 'the early warning system.' You can see what goes wrong in the U.S. and not repeat their worst follies." Trudeau, *Conversation with Canadians,* 128.

43 Gwyn, *Northern Magus,* 34.

44 Ricci, *Trudeau,* 84.

that of his upbringing. During the time he spent in Paris after Harvard, Trudeau adopted the religious philosophy of Personalism:

> a sort of spiritual existentialism, asserting the primacy of the individual and of free will but balancing these with the demands of social conscience and social responsibility. For Trudeau, the philosophy became – perhaps a bit conveniently – a means of both holding on to his past and of remaking it.[45]

He met leading Personalist philosopher Emmanuel Mounier in Paris and, more important, through his reading came under the influence of Nikolai Berdyaev, whom he mentions to McLuhan in his July 25, 1977, letter.

Although Trudeau lived a privileged life, which to some degree made him unable to relate to "ordinary" individuals, when he travelled as a young man he did not travel in privilege (except of course that he always had that family money to fall back on and did not really have to get a job). "Mean lives, the condition, after all, of much of the electorate, were not in his idiom. This is not to say that he didn't care, but that, on his part, it had to be an effort of will."[46] This perception of Trudeau as an elitist dogged him for his entire political career.

Herbert Marshall McLuhan was born in Edmonton on July 21, 1911, the elder son of Herbert McLuhan and Elsie Hall. On August 4, 1939, he married Texan Corinne Lewis in St. Louis; McLuhan had been teaching at the Jesuit Saint Louis University for two years. He and Corinne had six children. McLuhan died in Toronto on December 31, 1980, 15 months after a massive stroke left him unable to speak, read or write. From childhood, McLuhan had health problems, but viewed them as a sign of weakness and attempted to dismiss them. For almost eight years he tried to ignore the blackouts and dizziness that culminated in surgery from a benign brain tumour in 1967; it took him three years to recover.[47]

---

45 Ricci, *Trudeau*, 82.

46 Mordecai Richler, *Oh Canada! Oh Quebec!: Requiem for a Divided Country*. Toronto: Penguin Group, 1992, 158.

47 W. Terrence Gordon, *Marshall McLuhan: Escape into Understanding – A Biography*. New York: Basic Books, 1997, 226–230.

His life story, including his marriage and his background, could be a case study for a North America and a world where one could move around quite freely, formal international border controls such as visas and work permits still being relatively new developments. There were, however, passport difficulties in getting him and Corinne back from England after World War II broke out and, in 1943, he defended his dissertation *in absentia.*[48] During his graduate education at Cambridge, McLuhan travelled a lot, and he and Corinne also travelled on their honeymoon. But, in comparison to Trudeau, his travels were conventional and do not seem to have had much influence on his ideas.

McLuhan had a somewhat eclectic religious upbringing, exposed to several mainstream Protestant denominations. His mother even "dabbled in Christian Science and Rosicrucianism."[49] During his undergraduate years at the University of Manitoba in Winnipeg, McLuhan began reading the works of writer and Catholic convert G.K. Chesterton, whose significant influence on his thought and later on his writing style helped lead him to his own conversion to Catholicism while at Cambridge.

Margaret Trudeau was also a convert, though not by choice. I wonder whether she and McLuhan ever discussed the experience or whether the prime minister ever suggested that they do.

McLuhan was an active conservative Catholic for the rest of his life, attending Mass daily at St. Basil's Church on the campus of the University of St. Michael's College. St. Mike's, as it is known and as McLuhan referred to it in his September 29, 1971, letter to Davey, is a federated college of the University of Toronto and was McLuhan's academic home from 1946 until his death. He was an early "closet" follower of French Jesuit Pierre Teilhard de Chardin,[50] also an influence on Trudeau, who met him in Paris. Other mutual influences included the work of French Catholic philosopher Jacques Maritain.[51]

48 Gordon, *Marshall McLuhan,* 114.

49 Marchand, *Medium and Messenger,* 13.

50 Those who have cited Teilhard's influence include Jean-Francois Vallee [McLuhan100 Then Now Next: International Conference, Toronto, ON, November 7-10, 2011] and Tom Wolfe in http://www.marshallmcluhanspeaks.com.

51 Trudeau to McLuhan, July 25, 1977.

Teilhard remains controversial because of his views on basic Catholic teachings and his development of the theory of the noosphere, "a stage or sphere of evolutionary development characterized by (the emergence or dominance of) consciousness, the mind, and interpersonal relationships, postulated as following the stage of the establishment of human life."[52] For Trudeau, "The noosphere and individual rights (as distinguished from market capitalism) came together in [his] mind to make the global village that is Canada."[53] Maritain, who did much to revive 20th-century interest in Thomas Aquinas, developed a philosophy of liberal Christian humanism that included a defence of individual human rights. He lectured annually for many years at the University of Toronto's Pontifical Institute of Mediaeval Studies.

Right from the start, religion was part of the discussion between the professor and the politician. In his first letter to Trudeau, McLuhan wrote:

> I have always felt that one of Canada's greatest assets was its being a kind of "backwater". Never having been totally involved in current trends it has been able to enjoy a flexibility that is now rare. The rigidity of commitments of all Powers that were great in the 19th century confronts them with anarchy as they attempt to readjust to the total field awareness demanded by the speed of electric information. The de-Romanization of the Catholic Church is only one instance of the decentralizing effects of electric information on older bureaucracies. By the same token the liturgical revival is that kind of involvement and participation that goes with the simultaneity and coexistence of electronic experience.

The following year, McLuhan connected his thoughts on the Church to ideas about principles of organization, which took up more of his theoretical interest over the years and which were of practical concern to the prime minister as he figured out how best to organize his office and government. *Take Today: The Executive as Dropout*, McLuhan's 1972

52 http://www.oed.com.proxy.libraries.rutgers.edu/view/Entry/128215?redirectedFrom=noosphere#eid

53 Private email to me from B.W. Powe, March 8, 2017.

book written with international communications consultant Barrington Nevitt, is the McLuhan work cited most often in the Trudeau correspondence, though it has not loomed as large in his popular legacy. Always, McLuhan brought disparate ideas and systems together, writing to the prime minister on January 24, 1969, that

> In his new book 'The Age of Discontinuity' (Harper & Row, 1969), my friend Peter Drucker presents a magnificent inventory of problems in current decision making. He hasn't a clue as to why these problems have arisen but he cries out for a new theory of organization. He indicates that every organization in the world whether in the home or the school, the business or the political or the religious, has broken down today regardless of ideology or geography. On page 223 he focuses these problems onto the concept of the new 'ministate'. Every centralist organization large or small is now broken up into mini-states; even the Catholic individual, as he relates to the Mystical Body, regards himself as a mini-state.

McLuhan also never stopped thinking as someone from western Canada and took it upon himself as a Westerner to advise Trudeau on the subject; the western provinces presented many problems to the prime minister during his time in office. About one of the more theoretical issues, McLuhan informed the prime minister (July 10, 1973) that

> Last night's Toronto Star mentioned your having some doubts about the Canadian West and its strange attachment to the Mounties and the monarchy. As a Westerner, I can help to illuminate this matter. The West has always been on the defensive, if only because it is relatively uninhabited territory. Both the Mountie and the monarchy are figures, as it were, without a ground. They are lonely and isolated images, dedication without a cause.

But it was Canada as a whole, and Quebec in particular, that engaged McLuhan from the beginning of his relationship with Trudeau, even when his language lagged: by this time, the people of Quebec, the Québécois, had pretty much stopped using "French Canada" and "French-Canadian" when referring to themselves. In his first letter, he theorized that

> French Canada never had a 19th century. May this not be increasingly a basis for its great advantage over English Canada? Never having had the intense specialism of a mechanized consumer economy, French Canada retains its bonds with oral cultures and their total field approach. The all-at-oneness of electric data is not only organic and inclusive but reshapes the entire imaginative lives of highly literate communities. The TV generation, for example, is almost oriental in its involvement in the inner rather than the outer life. This means, naturally, a total loss of goal orientation in the old sense. The outer space programs thus in many ways represent 18th-century rather than 20th-century orientations.

Four years later, he wrote,

> I consider that Canada has become a world Utopia, as it were, by chance. Our unique situation seems to me to be that we are the only country in the world without an "identity." We have two identities which in effect polarize one another and create a very important pattern of complementarity. It is a complementarity of a special kind, deriving on the one hand from a great land power (France) and, on the other hand, a great sea power (England). Canada, in a most eminent way, embraces both of these cultural forms of land and sea.[54]

Whether through ego or playfulness, hunger to stand out or sheer forgetfulness, McLuhan's ideas, especially the dichotomy between hot and cool media, often seemed to contradict each other. Communications scholar Manuel Castells called him "the great visionary who revolutionized thinking in communications in spite of his unrestrained use

54 McLuhan to Trudeau, August 2, 1972. McLuhan had first mentioned to Trudeau in a December 2, 1968, letter his idea that Canada lacks a national identity.

of hyperbole."[55] The probe became McLuhan's basic *modus operandi.* When he used "the medium is the message" in his 1961–62 seminar class, he was testing out the ideas for both *The Gutenberg Galaxy* and, likely, *Understanding Media*, and was at that point using the phrase as a probe.[56]

McLuhan often used the line "You don't like my ideas? I have others."[57] But even if it is too much to expect McLuhan to be original from letter to letter or even book to book, he is extremely farsighted. One must not lose sight of the fact that he has been dead since 1980, before the age of even the personal computer, and that his work is not science, but a method of perception. McLuhan was not above playing with his cutting-edge image, however, telling Tom Wolfe in a 1970 TV-Ontario interview that "I've always been very careful never to predict anything that had not already happened. The future is not what it used to be."[58]

Although McLuhan, from the beginning, shared with Trudeau some of his core ideas about Canada, he was often ambivalent about both his native land and his adopted hometown. Tucked into the McLuhan files is a pamphlet for Sensory City '74, the 6th Conference on Visual Literacy, a meeting in Toronto which opened with a showing of the recent movie *The Apprenticeship of Duddy Kravitz*, set against the cultural frictions of Montreal's French, Jewish and English communities. A poem in the pamphlet reads

> Toronto is a city
> At the edge of
> American history....
> It is almost
> Tolkien's Rivendell
> Safe from the ragings
> Of the archaic darkness
> Of Sauron and the Ring Wraiths.[59]

---

55 Manuel Castells, *The Rise of the Network Society* (2nd ed.). Oxford: Blackwell, 2000, 357.

56 Surette [McLuhan100].

57 According to Antonio Casilli [McLuhan100 Then Now Next: International Conference, Toronto, ON, November 7-10, 2011], the first public use was in November 1955 at Columbia University.

58 http://www.marshallmcluhanspeaks.com

59 William Irwin Thompson, "At the Edge of History."

How much Canadian economic theorist Harold Innis influenced McLuhan and whether he expressed enough gratitude is a subject of continuing interest among McLuhan scholars and remains contentious. Certainly, McLuhan acknowledged Innis' understanding of interfaces, writing,

> Harold Innis, the Canadian pioneer historian of economics and communication, imaginatively used the interface, or borderline situation, to present a new world of economic and cultural change by studying the interplay between man's artifacts and the environments created by old and new technologies.[60]

Trudeau's *cri de coeur* asking for help dealt specifically with understanding the implications of the multiple kinds of identities coming to the fore in Canada at that same time. This need for help was practical, as Trudeau worked to develop national multiculturalism, but showed, at base, his desire to keep Canada whole. The fight for Canada, for Canadian federalism, across the softer boundaries of group identities but most especially across the real boundaries of Quebec and its culture, was the fight of Trudeau's adult life. At a private gathering in Toronto in November 1970, Trudeau

> remarked that national unity was not divinely ordained and that the country might break up some day. But the federation was far better for French Canadians than separation would be. He said that in the past he had sometimes played an intellectual game in which Quebec separated, so that people would see how much better off they had been in Confederation; but now that he was a politician with responsibilities for the people, he no longer played this game.[61]

Trudeau opposed the vision of Canada as the "community of communities" espoused by federal Progressive Conservative leader Joe Clark during the 1979 federal election campaign. He did view Canada as part

60 McLuhan, "Borderline Case," 233.

61 Cook, *Teeth of Time*, 114.

of a global community so that, should Quebec separate and the country fall apart, it would be "a crime against the history of mankind"[62] (often referenced as "a crime against humanity"). For Trudeau,

> the appeal of federalism [was] that it based itself not on ethnicity and emotionalism but on practicality and the common good. Trudeau may have come to this stance by way of the cauldron of his own crises of identity, but the reason he stuck with it was because it made sense. And if he had patched it together via Harvard and Harold Laski and China and the Khyber Pass, it was, in the end, a very Canadian stance.[63]

Neither McLuhan nor Trudeau worked at one job or even one single-minded career during their lifetimes, but lived roles utilizing a variety of skills. This change in customary expectations of work life came as no surprise to McLuhan, who said in a 1972 lecture that

> The work ethic, insofar as it meant private goal-orientation, is not practical and disappeared some time ago. Related to this situation is change in the job. The job will no longer hold up against the simultaneous jostling and the interfacing of simultaneous information. What is taking the place of the job is role-playing. When you are moonlighting and starlighting, that is role-playing; and most people are doing this to some degree or another. The job-holder drops out as the consultant drops in.[64]

He took up the subject directly with the prime minister a couple of years later (February 14, 1975), writing that

> The split between work and residence which came with industrial specialism and division of labour is ending swiftly with the new electric environment of software information.

62 John English, *Just Watch Me: The Life of Pierre Elliott Trudeau (1968–2000)*. Toronto: Alfred A. Knopf Canada, 2009, 332.

63 Ricci, *Trudeau*, 179.

64 Stephanie McLuhan and David Staines, eds., *Understanding Me: Lectures and Interviews*. Toronto: McClelland & Stewart, 2003, 189.

> The return to human scale and human involvement is getting spectacular play in the Thatcher episode, but it has also invaded the entire range of young people's attitudes and interests. Women's Lib belongs very much in the shift from specialist job-holding to multiple role-playing.

These role changes were a global phenomenon, which McLuhan had pointed out to Trudeau years earlier (January 24, 1969):

> Electric telecommunications create multitudes of tribally structured mini-states. These now begin to appear inside all the older maxi-states whether of business or politics. The unions and universities are mini-states, so are the police, the armed services, all media and all branches of business and government bureaucracies. The hierarchy of the organization chart is finished. Job specialism leads to role-playing in the global theatre.

I find McLuhan's ideas about tribalism useful in our globalizing world. He wrote (June 3, 1968) that

> The real drama of our age, the shift from hardware service environments of the 19th century to the software (electric information) service environments of the 20th century, is as big a leap as that from primitive tribalism to literate individualism. For our Western world, this is a shift from outer orientation to an inner, oriental trip. It renders all of our institutions obsolete, as the young TV generation fully recognizes...
>
> In these circumstances "political" action takes on the appearance of a paraplegic soccer match. It is not evident that any responsible figure in the Eastern or Western worlds has a clue to the erosion of human identity that follows upon the "software" environment. There is a corresponding release of violence to recover identity after technological innovation...

> Would not a high degree of awareness of these media effects (e.g. radio in Nigeria or in any tribal territory) enable us to set up social therapies and immunizing programs exactly comparable to medical action in the face of an endemic disease?

In one of their more playful discussions on this or any other subject, Trudeau wrote to McLuhan, somewhat tongue-in-cheek, that "I have always found fascinating your contention that the phonetic alphabet is a de-tribalizing influence, but the more I appear in print the less I am inclined to admit publicly your conclusion that schizophrenia is a necessary consequence of literacy." (November 7, 1968)

Six months later, McLuhan, who had sent Trudeau a tam and wanted to send him a matching kilt, noted, "The kilt, of course, is a mini-skirt, such as is worn by all tribal peoples. The mini-skirt is the same for men and women. Sex is not taken seriously by corporate societies. Hence the seeming nonsense of the hippies in this area." (May 29, 1969)

As years go by, the correspondence becomes increasingly marked up and copied – I don't know whether that is a sign of increased bureaucracy or deepening involvement. I have come across frequent references to the fact that, privately, Trudeau and McLuhan were good friends, but the correspondence does include some political advice about putting a bit of distance between them.

The relationship was encouraged, and initially mediated by, Davey, who had been instrumental in convincing Trudeau to run for the Liberal party leadership[65] and was himself attracted to McLuhan's ideas, which was not always good for the government. "Between 1968 and 1972, Davey was the architect both of Trudeau's ill-fated attempt to govern by reason, and by computers."[66] Davey's role as intermediary was not without complications. In an April 23, 1969, memo to Marc Lalonde, Trudeau's principal secretary, to arrange a meeting between Trudeau and McLuhan in Ottawa, Davey wrote, "I believe that Dr. McLuhan can be a source of valuable insights but, because he is a somewhat overpowering

65 Cook, *Teeth of Time*, 54.

66 Gwyn, *Northern Magus*, 84.

personality, the problem will be to find if any arrangements with him can be effective, and, if so, which."

Some of the issues Davey initially thought McLuhan might shed light on, during a proposed series of special seminars for government and political leaders, were these:

1) Priorities. What are they? How are they established? Does consensus form part of establishing priorities?

2) What is the role of a political party in today's electric age? The old and very slow ways of feeding information through the channels of local associations, provincial and national associations and M.P.s, etc., don't seem to me to have much continued relevance. How do we short-circuit this process but still maintain a "political party"?

3) What does Dr. McLuhan think about pluralistic societies or two-language societies?

4) What about the role of Canada versus the U.S. and Canada versus the world?

5) What is the future role for the United Nations?

6) Dr. McLuhan made some comments about the inadequacy of present education in the T.V. age. Does he have any solution to advocate?[67]

But the seminar series never materialized – the correspondence indicates that was due to a number of objections on McLuhan's part – and so, despite his continuing opinion that Trudeau could benefit from contact with the professor, Davey wrote in a memo to the prime minister (December 13, 1968) that "Dr. McLuhan may be too hard to handle if the contact is too frequent and too close. What would be helpful would be occasional correspondence and a lunch once or twice a year."

Brought in as a media specialist, McLuhan gave freely of his advice on the subject from the beginning of the relationship, writing on April 16, 1968, that

67 Davey memo to Senator Richard Stanbury, president of the Liberal Party of Canada, October 22, 1968.

> The men of the press can work only with people who have fixed points of view and definite goals, policies and objectives. Such fixed positions and attitudes are, of course, irrelevant to the electronic age. Our world substitutes mosaics for points of view and probes for targets.

"Understanding the proper use of the media and controlling one's exposure to it are, however, quite distinct as you will appreciate," replied Trudeau (November 25, 1969), a message that resonates even more vigorously now.

One of McLuhan's more well-known notions about Trudeau had to do with the idea of "mask," and he referred to it more than once in his writings to and about the prime minister.

> The very cool corporate mask that is your major political asset goes naturally with processing of problems in dialogue rather than in the production of packaged answers. That is why I urge you to go on the air with small groups and to trade problems with them rather than seeking answers or stating mere points of view.
>
> You are the only political image of our time able to use the T.V. medium without being forced to become a tribal buffoon or cartoon like De Gaulle. All the other political figures of the Western world are merely faded photographs on the T.V. medium. (January 24, 1969)

> Note how [President] Richard Nixon has ineptly tried to mitigate his crude and harsh image of liaison with various figures in the world of entertainment. He is quite unable to combine these qualities in himself in the way that you have done. To the Wasp world the light-hearted approach to power represents aristocratic insouciance and security. The entertainer is a figure which they themselves have crowned. He is permitted to hurt them by his humour, for that is the mask of his power and relevance alike. (February 12, 1973)

The idea could be misinterpreted, with some of Trudeau's critics taking it to mean that, beginning with Trudeau's run for the Liberal leadership, he had deliberately falsified his public image, which then fuelled what came to be known as Trudeaumania. "Your Grey Cup kick-off was, of course, a media triumph," McLuhan wrote. (December 2, 1968) "This is audience participation and image-making at its best."

> Your very cool dealings with our very hot medium the press, naturally produces intense interface or friction. The press has to have hot quotes and sharp points of view. Real news is bad news. Since the press lives on advertising, and all advertising is good news, it takes a lot of bad news to sell all this good news. Even the good news of the gospel can only be sold by hellfire. Vatican II made a very big mistake in this matter as in other matters.[68] (January 24, 1969)

Innovations in media and image-making would also work particularly well for Canada as a whole, according to McLuhan. Because Canada is unique on the world stage in never having had a national identity,

> In an age when all homogenous nations are losing their identity images through rapid technological change, Canada alone can "keep its cool." We have never been committed to a single course or goal. This is now our greatest asset. The parallel is to be found in the recent need of the business world to switch from private enterprise to tribal conglomerates on the pattern of medieval dynastic marriages, another massive example of decentralism foisted upon us by electric speeds. (December 2, 1968)

We live at a time when it's often a luxury to not be hooked in, to go off the grid, which gives both Trudeau's way of life and McLuhan's

68 On February 20, 1970, McLuhan wrote publisher Frank Sheed that "There was nobody at Vatican I or II who showed any understanding of the electro-technical thing in reshaping the psyche and culture of mankind... [T]he Catholic bureaucracy has moved resolutely into the 19th century, supported by plain-clothed priests and nuns. If a few people could only stop asking whether this is "a good thing or a bad thing" and spend some time in studying what is really happening, there might be some possibility of achieving relevance." Molinaro, Corinne McLuhan and Toye, eds., *Letters,* 399.

fears a kind of prescience. As one writer noted in *The New York Times* several years ago,

> The future of travel, I'm reliably told, lies in "black-hole resorts," which charge high prices precisely because you can't get online in their rooms...
>
> Even half a century ago, Marshall McLuhan, who came closer than most to seeing what was coming, warned, "When things come at you very fast, naturally you lose touch with yourself."[69]

Disconnecting on vacation comes at a premium in a world where, for most people, constantly connecting has become ordinary. In the air especially, we can travel at great speeds, out of touch with the earth, until we reach our destination and slow down to get back in touch with ourselves.

Thinking about globalization in terms of communications and transportation, I begin to try to hold two ideas in my head at the same time, the same way I puzzle over light being both wave and particle. When I'm on a plane, leafing through the airline's magazine, and see a drawing of the company's routes across the US or the world, I'm both amazed at the short distances and aware that, even when the lines are drawn straight, the real flights must take into account the curvature of the planet. Time-space compression makes us think of globalization as connecting nations, groups and individuals in straight and increasingly short and speedy lines. Yet we know the earth is in fact a globe and its shape determines forces or nature we can't change. Humans still have to move in real time and space and are constrained by circumstances – economics, violence, laws backed by police or military enforcement – in ways that information, agricultural products and durable goods may not be. Geographic proximity – how close home is to where home is going to be – and the existence of family members or others from home in the new location are two of the three main reasons determining where people move when they move,[70] though such decision-making

69 http://www.nytimes.com/2012/01/01/opinion/sunday/the-joy-of-quiet.html

70 Richard Langhorne, *The Essentials of Global Politics*. London: Hodder Arnold, 2006, 304.

for refugees, who are escaping, is not often as neat as for those migrating by choice.

Even in this globalizing world, Canada still is very tied to its geography, as is every other nation state, each in its own way. But global communications technology can provide synthesis.

> The question of identifying national borders on the internet is complicated by the fact that there is no clear agreement as to what 'national borders' are... A traditional view of the national border suggests itself as a starting point. In this conception, a national border is an imaginary boundary tied strictly to geographical territory in which a state's sovereignty may be exercised... While such a definition is well suited to discussions between national governments, determining the sovereignty of nations by their territorial borders does not account for two vital ingredients of a nation: its people and their culture. People have always made connections across national borders, but improvements in communication and transportation technologies have made such connections far easier as the 20th century comes to a close. A political or legal sense of national borders ignores, by and large, these vital connections.[71]

Canada is not only a middle land – it is also a middle power. In the early 1900s, the technology required for new forms of popular culture, such as movies, "required either government assistance or enormous markets [so] Canadians fell increasingly under the influence of the United States."[72] As Canada struggled to find its independent voice after WWII, having been fully in control of its own foreign affairs only since the passage of the Statute of Westminster in 1931, Canadian officials stuck to the same "functional principle" they had stuck to during WWII:

> [R]epresentation in the United Nations' councils only when Canada could be a major actor. In allocating supplies or feeding refugees, Canadians must have a voice; on grand

71 Alexander Halavais, "National Borders on the World Wide Web." *New Media & Society* 2:1 (2000): 7–28, at 8.

72 Craig Brown, ed., *The Illustrated History of Canada*. Toronto: Lester & Orpen Dennys, 1987, 442.

> strategy, they would be silent... Between the great powers, bent on monopolizing decision-making, and a host of minor countries with voices but no leverage, Canada was a "middle power" with too little influence to claim a global voice but with too great a material strength to be ignored.[73]

McLuhan took some delight in teasing Americans, telling Trudeau,

> While attending the idiotic Bilderbung Conference[74] on world unrest I spoke to George Ball of the U.S. I said: "The Canadians are a very cool crowd." He replied: "Not according to my mail." I asked him: "What was the cause for irritation?" He then explained his plan for taking over Canada. I replied: "Well, Mr. Ball, to be quite frank, I have not only never heard of your plan, but I have never heard of you before in my life. Why don't you all come up and live on the Dew Line which you have built? All Americans could live up there without even being noticed!" (May 29, 1969)

Trudeau has never gone out of style, especially for me, although there has been more criticism of his politics over the years. As recently as 2014, Trudeau topped a poll which asked, "Which Canadians have inspired you most over the last 150 years?"[75]

And there has been quite a McLuhan revival in this century, though also not free of detractors. Minimally, his influence continues to be felt and his works cited, even when his name is not specifically invoked. He has even achieved cartoon immortality of a sort. In an episode of TV's *Family Guy*,[76] fittingly titled "A Picture is Worth 1,000 Books," King Neptune says, "You know nothing of my work," the same line of dialogue Woody Allen gave McLuhan in the movie *Annie Hall* and that Douglas

---

73 Brown, *The Illustrated History of Canada*, 484–485.

74 Given the disdain McLuhan shows here for the conference, it is probably intentional that he referred to it as Bilderbung, rather than Bilderberg. The invitation-only Bilderberg Conferences have been held annually since 1954. In April 1968, it was held in Mont Tremblant, Quebec, and I think this is the event to which he is referring.

75 http://www.cbc.ca/news/canada/top-10-canadian-heroes-list-includes-pierre-trudeau-jack-layton-1.2676398

76 The episode (season 2, episode 11) first aired on April 18, 2000.

Coupland used for his biography.[77] These days, I find it hard to argue with McLuhan's point, albeit overstated, that "Terror is the normal state of any oral society, for in it everything affects everything"[78] or that "One of the many flips of our time is that the electric information environment returns man to the condition of the most primitive prober and hunter. Privacy invasion is now one of our biggest knowledge industries."[79]

Trudeau's influence is also still felt, though maybe not globally right now, except through some renewed fascination because of Justin's recent political success, shining particularly brightly on the world stage with his policies of welcoming refugees and legalizing marijuana. "Trudeau" is often the only Canadian whose name Americans and other non-Canadians recognize when I mention it, and McLuhan is routinely thought of, if recognized at all in similar casual moments, as American.

Post–Expo '67 optimism about Canada's greatness was premature. On the world stage, Canada is still the props guy – resource-full, good at particular skills, indispensable backstage. McLuhan wrote,

> Since the United States has become a world environment, Canada has become the anti-environment that renders the United States more acceptable and intelligible to many small countries of the world; anti-environments are indispensable for making an environment understandable.[80]

Occasionally, Canada is floated in the media as a cautionary tale – for example, in the months leading up to the failed Scottish bid for independence from the United Kingdom in 2014 and in some of the analyses immediately afterward. But in 1968, when McLuhan, the globally renowned media guru, connected to Trudeau, Canada's new political superstar, anything seemed possible.

> [N]ot only were McLuhan and Trudeau frequent correspondents and dinner companions, they were definitely electronic-era soulmates. While McLuhan was one of the

77 Douglas Coupland, *Marshall McLuhan: You Know Nothing of My Work*. New York: Atlas & Co., 2010.

78 Marshall McLuhan, *The Gutenberg Galaxy*. Toronto: University of Toronto Press, 1962, 32.

79 McLuhan, *Culture*, 24.

80 McLuhan, "Borderline Case," 227.

> first communications experts to recognize that the content of the mass media was infinitely less meaningful than its form, Trudeau was one of the first Canadian politicians to make politics seem vastly less important than persona.[81]

McLuhan presciently described a world in which communications technologies would become so radically different that everyone everywhere would be connected to each other like villagers:

> The tribe is a unit, which, extending the bounds of the family to include the whole society, becomes the only way of organizing society when it exists in a kind of Global Village pattern. It is important to understand that the Global Village pattern is caused by the instantaneous movement of information from every quarter to every point at the same time.[82]

Information would be known globally, and that would shape the world, which would also shape the information, an echo of Winston Churchill's "We shape our buildings, and afterwards our buildings shape us."[83] Some television viewers today accept payment to allow TV monitoring companies to install a device on their televisions that tracks their eye movements as they watch, to help companies design more effective commercials.[84]

McLuhan's global villagers were meant to be better connected to each other, but to stay in place. Despite his enthusiasm for Buckminster Fuller's Spaceship Earth,[85] he may not have imagined the contemporary argument that "since a large part of our lives are now spent online, our offline selves ought to enjoy the same degree of fluidity, and that global

81 Geoff Pevere and Greig Dymond, *Mondo Canuck: A Canadian Pop Culture Odyssey*. Scarborough: Prentice-Hall Canada, 1996, 223.

82 Letter from McLuhan to Edward S. Morgan, May 16, 1959. This can be considered his first use of "global village." Molinaro, Corinne McLuhan and Toye, eds., *Letters*, 252.

83 http://www.winstonchurchill.org/learn/speeches/quotations/famous-quotations-and-stories

84 https://www.nytimes.com/2017/02/25/business/media/tv-viewers-tracking-tools.html?_r=0

85 Richard Buckminster "Bucky" Fuller (1895–1983), architect and innovator, coined the term "Spaceship Earth."

or world citizenship isn't as much of a utopian ideal as it is a technological and historical inevitability."[86]

His idea that the (generation) gap is where the action is continues to have much global relevance in a world trying to understand ungoverned spaces and in the rise of violence committed by youth in those spaces and others. In an early letter to Trudeau (June 3, 1968), McLuhan wrote, "The TV kids cannot accept the identity of their parents' generation so they will simply destroy any institutional or legal attempt to impose it upon them."

In a post-9/11 world of ascendant youth, in which more migrants are trying to move more places for more reasons, including environmental degradation, walls are going up along borders or being proposed or, in Europe, being reconsidered. The governing powers of Canada and the US have been steadily and sometimes stealthily melting their joint border, with security operations being set up further and further into each other's country.[87]

Writing of the other North American border, the one with Mexico – and, increasingly, what is meant by "the border" in popular American culture, as Canada continues to lose ground – one author writes,

> The only problem is, as Jacques Derrida says, the closer we get to the border, the harder it gets to see it. Reality blurs. Uncertainty becomes a principle.
>
> If you focus on that blurred border, you begin to understand that Spanglish is so much more than reading between the lines... At the border, an obvious and often awkward mixing of cultures takes place that makes up the superficial idea of Spanglish. But the border also exists deep within the territory of North America, now more than ever, in its major cities; it is an imported border that is expressed through a dynamic, continuing recombination of cultures.[88]

86 Abrahamian, *Cosmopolites,* 115.

87 A relatively recent example, in which American intrusion into Canada was marketed and supported by politicians of many stripes, involves expedited border crossings: http://www.cbc.ca/news/politics/border-clearance-us-passes-1.3891092.

88 Ed Morales, *Living in Spanglish: The Search for Latino Identity in America.* New York: St. Martin's Press, 2002, 4.

That recombination of cultures also occurs, less benignly, inside the corridors of power. A mid-2016 summit of the Canadian, US and Mexican leaders dealt with proposals for increased efficiency of border crossings, including data sharing, and the embedding of Canadian personnel alongside Mexican counterparts in a US customs centre to fight the illegal smuggling of contraband goods with better pre-screening for high-risk cargo shipments: "The three countries will embrace 'cluster asset mapping,' to identify regions with interconnected companies, suppliers and institutions... They will also cooperate on cybersecurity."[89]

Generally, Americans notice Canadians only if they are momentarily perceived as a threat to security and notice Mexicans as a threat to national culture, while misperceiving them as a threat to the domestic economy and national security.

Still, in March 2016, there was a moment of hope in the gap between that reality and whatever the upcoming US presidential election would bring, when Prime Minister Justin Trudeau stood beside President Barack Obama at a joint press conference and heard him say,

> And so, working together to find effective ways – not to close off borders, not to pretend that somehow we can shut off trade, not to forget that we are, ourselves, nations of immigrants and that diversity is our strength – but rather to say, yes, the world is big and we are going to help shape it, and we're going to value our openness and our diversity, and the fact that we are leaders in a global supply chain but we're going to do so in ways that make sure everybody benefits – that's important work that we're going to have to do together.[90]

The candle burns at both ends and yet, for a resonating interval, the centre holds.

---

89 http://www.cbc.ca/news/politics/three-amigos-agreements-list-1.3658050

90 https://www.whitehouse.gov/the-press-office/2016/03/10/remarks-president-obama-and-prime-minister-trudeau-canada-joint-press

The Letters

1968

April 16, 1968[91]

Hon. Pierre Trudeau
Minister of Justice
Ottawa, Ontario, Canada

Dear Pierre Trudeau:

It was a piece in the Toronto *Telegram* by Douglas Fisher and Harry Crowe that emboldened me to drop you a note. The piece was entitled Good Will for Trudeau, for a time.

The men of the press can work only with people who have fixed points of view and definite goals, policies and objectives. Such fixed positions and attitudes are, of course, irrelevant to the electronic age. Our world substitutes mosaics for points of view and probes for targets. Knowing of your acquaintance with De Tocqueville,[92] I can understand why you have such an easy understanding of the North American predicament in the new electronic age. The U.S.A., in particular, began with

91 When there are differences in punctuation or spelling between the originals and the letters as they appear in the *Letters of Marshall McLuhan*, edited by Matie Molinaro, Corinne McLuhan and William Toye and published by Oxford University Press in 1987, I use the original. However, many typos and spelling mistakes have been corrected for this book. The Oxford version of this letter indicates that it was written in Bronxville, NY, where McLuhan lived during his year at Fordham University. The original was written on university stationery. McLuhan wrote almost all of his letters to Trudeau from Toronto and Trudeau answered from Ottawa, so I have left that information off most of the correspondence.

92 Alexis de Tocqueville (1805–1859), French political thinker and historian.

the latest technology, namely, printing from movable type. The dynamics of that process inspired and permeated the entire industrial and social establishment that grew so rapidly and consistently between 1776 and the present. Any "backward" country tends to enjoy the advantage of starting with the latest technology, so that in the electric age, all the countries that missed the 19th century and its mechanical orientation can now speedily adapt to electric technology without endangering any literate and mechanistic backlog of achievement, e.g. Russia, Japan, etc.

French Canada never had a 19th century.[93] May this not be increasingly a basis for its great advantage over English Canada? Never having had the intense specialism of a mechanized consumer economy, French Canada retains its bonds with oral cultures and their total field approach. The all-at-onceness of electric data is not only organic and inclusive but reshapes the entire imaginative lives of highly literate communities. The TV generation, for example, is almost oriental in its involvement in the inner rather than the outer life. This means, naturally, a total loss of goal orientation in the old sense. The outer space programs thus in many ways represent 18th century rather than 20th century orientations.

McLuhan had astute ideas about the effects of a nation bypassing a technology. Today, for example:

> **In China, what is sometimes called "the shift to mobile" never happened – hasn't needed to happen – because the country's wealth is too recent for people to have been swept up in the PC revolution, the way Americans were. Instead, they went straight to phones, an example of a phenomenon known as leapfrogging, in which non-participation in an older technology spurs early adoption of whatever innovation comes next. Jack Ma, of Alibaba, has argued that the entire e-commerce sector in China exemplifies this pattern: people happily shop online because there haven't been Walmarts everywhere.**

https://www.newyorker.com/magazine/2018/07/23/how-e-commerce-is-transforming-rural-china

93 This sentence has been underlined, presumably by Trudeau, as were "Any backward" and "tends to enjoy the advantage of starting" in the previous paragraph.

I have always felt that one of Canada's greatest assets was its being a kind of "backwater". Never having been totally involved in current trends it has been able to enjoy a flexibility that is now rare. The rigidity of commitments of all Powers that were great in the 19th century confronts them with anarchy as they attempt to readjust to the total field awareness demanded by the speed of electric information. The de-Romanization of the Catholic Church is only one instance of the decentralizing effects of electric information on older bureaucracies. By the same token the liturgical revival is that kind of involvement and participation that goes with the simultaneity and coexistence of electronic experience.

At present I am studying the American political developments, noting the utter conflict between Policies and Images as it concerns the candidates. May not the same thing happen here as in Canada recently? The old political professionals simply exhaust and liquidate themselves by going through the old motions, making room for quite unexpected candidates at the last moment.

Like most Canadians, I am delighted that it happened that way for us and that you are to enter into this complex new role.

With most cordial wishes and prayers,
Marshall McLuhan

May 21, 1968

Dear Dr. McLuhan:

I am writing on behalf of the Prime Minister to thank you for your very kind letter of April 16th.

The Prime Minister had asked me to call you personally but, unfortunately, I was unable to reach you on the occasions I tried. The Prime Minister was most interested in your comments and, if I may add, so was I. We discussed them on several occasions and, in a recent speech to an audience of broadcasters, he mentioned a number of the ideas that you had expressed to him in your letter.

I know that in more leisurely times after the present election campaign, he is looking forward to the opportunity of meeting you.

May I thank you, therefore, once again on his behalf.

Yours sincerely,
J. M. Davey

June 3, 1968

Dear Pierre Trudeau:

After seeing the Kennedy-McCarthy "debate",[94] I wish that you were not going to be on TV at all. It is not a debating medium.[95]

Trying to formulate the chances of the American candidates for publication, I can find only one word: "somnambulism."

It was Professor Broughton of McGill[96] who recently explained that somnambulism is a highly motivated state.

The real drama of our age, the shift from hardware service environments of the 19th century to the software (electric information) service environments of the 20th century, is as big a leap as that from primitive tribalism to literate indi-

The first political leaders' debate in a Canadian election campaign was held on June 9. Bobby Kennedy's assassination three days earlier cast a pall over the proceedings, and the stilted format, as McLuhan had predicted earlier, was generally seen as boring and inconclusive.

https://en.wikipedia.org/wiki/1968_Canadian_federal_election

A clipping in the McLuhan archives: A June 10, 1968, front page from the *Toronto Star* had a lead story about the debate; in a photo in a black-bordered box to the left of that story, Ethel Kennedy and one of her sons stand beside Robert Kennedy's grave.

---

94 The US Democratic presidential primary debate between Senators Robert Kennedy and Eugene McCarthy had been broadcast on ABC-TV two days earlier.

95 This sentence has been underlined, presumably by Trudeau. He did not debate during the 1980 election campaign. Trudeau, *Memoirs,* 269.

96 Likely Dr. Roger J. Broughton: https://www.bristolwhoswho.com/bristol-whos-who-recognizes-dr-roger-j-broughton.

vidualism. For our Western world, this is a shift from outer orientation to an inner, oriental trip. It renders all of our institutions obsolete, as the young TV generation fully recognizes. (The TV generation is now 12 to 14 years of age and hasn't reached the college plateau yet).

In these circumstances "political" action takes on the appearance of a paraplegic soccer match. It is not evident that any responsible figure in the Eastern or Western worlds has a clue to the erosion of human identity that follows upon the "software" environment. There is a corresponding release of violence to recover identity after technological innovation.[97] The TV kids cannot accept the identity of their parents' generation so they will simply destroy any institutional or legal attempt to impose it upon them. The liquidation of the feudal system with the advent of printing and gunpowder represented a very slow change from corporate to private identity, compared to the reverse of that process that we are now undergoing.

Radio created Hitler as a delinquent Peter Pan, charged with cosmic emanation.

Would not a high degree of awareness of these media effects (e.g. radio in Nigeria or in any tribal territory) enable us to set up social therapies and immunizing programs exactly comparable to medical action in the face of an endemic disease?

Pardon me for feeling very uncomfortable in the presence of what is called "political" discussion in circumstances such as these.

Cordial good wishes for June 9.
Marshall McLuhan

June 12, 1968

Dear Pierre Trudeau:

I was shown the video tape of the great debate in Toronto on Monday and taped a comment to be used later by CFTO.[98]

97 Most of this sentence has been underlined.

98 CFTO in Toronto is the flagship station of the CTV television network in Canada.

The witness box cum lectern cum pulpit spaces for the candidates was totally non-TV. I had not seen you or Stanfield[99] before. Stanfield's image is that of the Yankee horsetrader, as shrewd as sabbatical or hebdomadal. I gather he is a distant relative of mine. My mother's people came from the same territory. Nova Scotia is one of the most Yankee parts of North America. Boston is the cultural capital still. The other side of Stanfield is "Honest Abe" --- the vote splitter.

Your own image is a corporate mask, inclusive, requiring no private nuance whatever. This is your "cool" TV power. Iconic, sculptural. A mask "puts on" an audience. At a masquerade we are not private persons.

Your book on Federalism[100] is at the Edmund Burke[101] level. My favorite quote from him is: "The first right of every man in civilized society is the right to be protected against the consequences of his own stupidity."

The cover of the June 8-14 TV Guide is a Dali masterpiece.[102] It manifests in detail the tactile quality of the TV image. The extension of the central nervous system via electricity is environmentally indicated in the upper right corner by a

One example of the continuing relevance of McLuhan's ideas about the extensions of man (or, today, humans):

> **"The behavior of the Millennial generation is not infrequently criticized, especially regarding their relationship to technology. But if Millennials live their lives via screens, says Lewis Black, it's because the Baby Boomer generation gave them digital technology like an unsought after acid trip: 'That generation turns around and drops on these kids something that was just as potent as LSD. That phone and the amount of apps and the amount of crap and the computer, it's the extension of the human nervous system.'"**
>
> http://bigthink.com/videos/lewis-black-on-the-millennials-and-the-baby-boomers?utm_campaign=Echobox&utm_medium=Social&utm_source=Facebook#link_time=1457316238

99 Robert Stanfield was Leader of the Opposition in Parliament, as head of the Progressive Conservative Party, from 1967 to 1976.

100 *Federalism and the French Canadians*, a selection of Trudeau's writings, published in 1967.

101 Edmund Burke, political philosopher (1729–1797).

102 The cover story in that issue of *TV Guide* was titled "Salvador Dali's view of television." http://www.daliblog.com/DaliTV2.jpg. I find the cover off-putting and desolate.

segment of brain tissue. The two thumbs with the TV images on the nails are carefully separated to indicate the "gap" or interval constituted by touch. The age of tactility via television and radio is one of innumerable interfaces or "gaps" that replace the old connections, legal, literate and visual.

Very best wishes,
[M.M.]

June 19, 1968

Dear Mr. Davey:

Just a note apropos the name "Trudeau". It doesn't mean only "water hole" but Tour d'eau or "water tower", a more striking image.

Sincerely yours,
[M.M.]

McLuhan had asked his friend, artist René Cera, for help with the derivation of "Trudeau." Cera answered on April 20, 1968, that "Off hand, purely on ordinary grounds, I would say that 'Trudeau' might be a deformation of Trou-d'eau or Water-hole – or again, Tour-d'eau or Water Tower. Just from memory I cannot discover any sort of clue to the exact meaning of 'Tru' – unless I accept 'In|trus' (intruse) which by 'extension' would give In-truding – as a possible substitute. ???"

July 3rd 1968.

Dear Mr. McLuhan:

Please accept my sincere thanks for your two books, "Explorations" and "Pour comprendre les médias," which you were kind enough to inscribe for me.

I am very pleased to have these volumes for my library.

Yours sincerely,

Ever since our brief exchange in Charlottetown, June 1964, I have been hoping we might meet again.

P.

Trudeau led the federal Liberals to a majority win on June 25, taking 154 of the 264 seats in the House of Commons at the time and more than 45 percent of the popular vote.

***Explorations in Communication*, co-edited with media studies colleague and anthropologist Edmund "Ted" Snow Carpenter, had been published in 1960.**

The French translation of McLuhan's 1964 book, *Understanding Media: The Extensions of Man*, was published in 1968. *Understanding Media* contained the core of McLuhan's thinking and marked the high point of his career.

The note about meeting again is handwritten. Biographers Clarkson and McCall place Trudeau in Charlottetown to speak at the annual meeting of the Canadian Political Science Association.

July 10, 1968

Dear Dr. McLuhan:

Thank you very much for your note of June 19th concerning the origin of the name "Trudeau". I was indeed intrigued with the idea that it meant "Water Tower".

I have read with very great interest all your letters to the Prime Minister, particularly the one with the list of "Icons." As a physicist myself and someone who has been working in the computer field for the past 15 years and now finds himself participating in the political process, I am very stimulated indeed with the ideas raised by your letters as well as by your books.

I am personally looking forward to an opportunity of meeting with you, which I hope will be soon.

Yours sincerely,
Jim Davey.

September 27, 1968

Dear Mr. Prime Minister:

The New York Times suddenly tossed this opportunity my way to write a brief review of your book. I hope it will not displease you. I did, of course, intend to tease the Americans.

Sincerely yours,[103]
H M McLuhan

The Trudeau archives include a photocopy of the December 7, 1968, Canadian Press wire story in the *Ottawa Citizen* ("McLuhan Praises PM"), discussing the review, which was filled with puns and references to many McLuhanisms current at the time or soon to come into fuller bloom. It was effusive in its analysis of Trudeau, "the Man in the Mask" who "grew up straddling two cultures, perfectly at home in both."

October 17, 1968

Dear Mr. Prime Minister:

Bill Lee[104] happens to be here at present and is en route to Ottawa and I take this opportunity to have him bring this letter to you directly in order to expedite matters.

103 There is a handwritten note on the page, from Jim Davey to Trudeau, reading "P.M. I'm not sure I understand the review, but I'm prepared to attempt a 'tease' acknowledgement should you wish me to. Jim." An answering note on the page reads "please do" and is initialled by the prime minister.

104 Bill Lee was a political consultant who became Trudeau's campaign manager after running the Liberal leadership campaign of rival Paul Hellyer. The Hellyer campaign was noted as the first to use a computer to track delegates.

Naturally, I hope you were pleased with last night's affair. This letter concerns it immediately. After you and your colleagues had left, Dick Stanbury, Bob McCormick and myself were chatting. It occurred to us that a strategy that might encompass the entire program of "participational democracy" might be mounted as follows: the student power groups in high schools and colleges are available as a Canadian mosaic. If you could chat with the leaders of such groups on TV (four or five at a time) it would itself be participation in the highest levels of government, since these people represent one of the principal problems of government today.

The answer to their problems, as we discussed it last night, does not consist in plugging them into some existing bureaucracy, whether of high school or of college. They are not looking for "feed-back" but "feed-forward." It would be inevitable that as soon as they began to discuss their problems there would begin a resonance with many problems of your own. It would be perfectly natural for you to illustrate and to discuss their problems while briefing them on yours. They in turn could comment on yours, setting up a natural interface between areas of community life on one hand, and government on the other. Such an encounter via TV has never occurred before.

That same day, the Official Languages Act was introduced in Parliament. The Act, which passed the following July, made both French and English the official languages of Canada, guaranteeing the right to use either language in all federal institutions and services. The intent of the Act "was to give legislative effect to Trudeau's belief that only when the French and English languages were given equal protection as working languages at the federal level would French Canadians come to look upon the Canadian government as their own." (Cook, *Teeth of Time*, 202.)

Yet somehow, the night before this critical event, Trudeau had made the time to drop in at a strategy meeting with McLuhan, a number of advisors, Liberal politicians, Davey and others.

During such discussions (and let me suggest that there be no studio audience whatever) your own natural, easy, flexible way would relax them and alert them to many features of the world in which they live, in a totally new way.

Just as the gap between culture and business has closed by virtue of an electric information environment, so the gap between politics and youth has closed. Teenagers are no longer young persons mentally or emotionally. Indeed, part of their dilemma consists in being categorized as teenagers or as youngsters. The immediate consequence of such a political education strategy would be to remove an enormous burden from the backs of educational administrators and parents alike. They, too, could enjoy the immediate sensation of participating in problems at the highest level. The merely parochial aspects of their dilemmas would vanish.

The time is long overdue for you to be back in circulation and to be in the Canadian living room as a "gap-bridger", the unifying image of our society that you became during the election.[105] It is impossible to exaggerate the advantages in political education that would result. "Government of the air" would by-pass all bureaucracy yet make it possible to consider the problems of bureaucracies of all kinds. Data from government departments could be brought to bear in follow-up sessions. Perhaps it might be more effective to canvass various features of this kind of program by telephone.

I am prepared to contact the leaders of the student activists on this campus to invite you at once to appear with them on such a program. No preliminary briefing or scripting of any kind would be necessary or desirable. All protocol could be tossed aside. I feel confident that the obvious obstacles to this innovation can be by-passed. This kind of political mountain-climbing could be done in spite of all the obvious road-blocks. The program would not only be a political one but an educational one so far as the C.B.C. is concerned.

Medium-mystically yours,
Marshall McLuhan

105 This sentence has been emphasized by some reader with two vertical lines in the left margin.

November 7, 1968

Dear Professor McLuhan,

Jacques Hébert, whom Trudeau appointed to the Senate in 1983, co-founded Katimavik in 1977, a volunteer program for university-age Canadians which helped them learn about each other across cultures and language barriers.

Thank you for your courtesy in sending to me your review. The assorted launching activities which seem to be an integral part of the current commercial publishing process are quickly persuading me that you are wrong – that the publication is not performance, rather that the act of publication is a performance.

I have always found fascinating your contention that the phonetic alphabet is a de-tribalizing influence, but the more I appear in print the less I am inclined to admit publicly your conclusion that schizophrenia is a necessary consequence of literacy. In any event, some of the consequences of the reappearance of my China book[106] have led me to wonder if I was wrong in permitting it to appear in other than ideographic form. Does that mean I have lost my equilibrium?

The proposal in your letter of October 17 concerning a television appearance with student leaders is a provocative one; I have asked that it be considered for possible inclusion in my future programme. Thank you for your suggestion.

Yours sincerely,
[P.E.T.]

November 13, 1968

Dear Mr. Prime Minister:

Just a note about media strategy. In your discussion with students from the floor, shown on "The Way It Is"[107] last Sunday, November 10th, you could not have been in a more dangerous position media-wise.

106 *Two Innocents in Red China*, co-authored with Jacques Hébert, one of a small group of close Trudeau friends who travelled together to China in 1960. The book was originally written in French and published in 1961 as *Deux innocents en Chine rouge*.

107 A public affairs program broadcast on CBC from 1967 to 1969.

An auditorium violates the very nature of TV, hence the disaster of the political conventions in the U.S.A. Television demands close, casual, intimate discussions. Also no notes, no script, and no debating. The discernment and conception of process prompts total avoidance of debating. The process by which the business community is switched from private goals to conglomerate inter-marriage is identical with the process of decentralism and participation which all students demand of their institutions today. The same process has deprived students of their identity. The loss of identity and goals in the political and business spheres causes the same indiscriminate resort to violent struggle.

Paradoxically, the business community demands a "double standard." While making rapid adjustments to changing technologies, it expects the educational and political establishments to remain rigidly fixed in the old patterns. This is the result of visual classification which avoids the awareness of function and process.

In my War and Peace book[108] I explain how technological change deprives individuals and societies of their identity images, with resulting struggle for new images. In Through the Vanishing Point (which I am taking the liberty of sending you), Harley Parker[109] and I explain how many new kinds of space, psychic and social, result from technological change.

Most cordial good wishes,
[M.M.]

November 25, 1968

Dear Professor McLuhan:

Thank you for sending to me a copy of your fascinating new book (I had never thought of abstract art as marking the end of visual space;

108 *War and Peace in the Global Village*, written with frequent collaborator Quentin Fiore and published in 1968.

109 Marshall McLuhan and Harley Parker, *Through the Vanishing Point: Space in Poetry and Painting*. New York: Harper & Row, 1968. Canadian artist Parker was McLuhan's colleague from 1967 to 1975 at the Centre for Culture and Technology at the University of Toronto.

the suggestion is an intriguing one) and for your views on the most effective employment of TV. Understanding the proper use of the media and controlling one's exposure to it are, however, quite distinct as you will appreciate.

The identity process of which you speak so often is one that cannot be ignored by government. I am very much aware of the sometimes search and sometimes struggle for new images in which many communities of our society are engaging. What I lack is an intuitive process to forecast for me the likeliest form of a satisfactory nature which these new images will assume. Can you help me?

Yours sincerely,
Pierre E. Trudeau

December 2, 1968

Dear Mr. Prime Minister:

Miss McDermott of your new Information Task Force has contacted me. She will be coming to participate in our media seminar at the Centre[110] tonight (we meet every Monday evening from 8 to 10).

I wish I had much more time to be of help. I still have a full academic program and I am still convalescing from the brain surgery of one year ago. It is this latter fact that restricts my travels.

My forte is structural analysis of new problems and environments that, unawares to us, re-program our sensory lives. In effect I am saying that it is now possible to by-pass what used to be called "fate" by anticipating the effects of new man-made environments.

Naturally this concerns every level of our personal and political lives. I am therefore very eager to be of help to you. Perhaps we can invent a way of making this possible within the severe limits imposed upon your time. Do you think the telephone a practical possibility? Would a personal representative of yourself, visiting me here, be another possibility?

110 The Centre for Culture and Technology.

Your Grey Cup[111] kick-off was, of course, a media triumph. This is audience participation and image-making at its best. Fire-side dialogues with small groups of students would be even more potent.

One theme that may have some immediate relevance: Canada is the only country in the world that has never had a national identity. In an age when all homogenous nations are losing their identity images through rapid technological change, Canada alone can "keep its cool." We have never been committed to a single course or goal. This is our greatest asset. The parallel is to be found in the recent need of the business world to switch from private enterprise to tribal conglomerates on the pattern of medieval dynastic marriages, another massive example of decentralism foisted upon us by electric speeds.

With cordial good wishes and prayers for your welfare,
Marshall McLuhan

December 13, 1968

MEMORANDUM FOR THE PRIME MINISTER VIA MR. LALONDE

From: J. M. Davey

Re: Marshall McLuhan

Attached is a letter from Dr. McLuhan and a suggested reply. The periodic comments from Dr. McLuhan have been fascinating and often illuminating. He is a man of immense capacity and great gifts of insight, but he is far enough out in the future that it is difficult to discuss usefully current problems with him. I believe that we can get the greatest value from the horizons that he can open to our thinking rather than illumination of the path immediately ahead.

Perhaps you think otherwise, but I believe that Dr. McLuhan may be hard to handle if the contact is too frequent and too close. What would

111 The most important annual football game in Canada, named for the silver trophy donated in 1909 by Governor General Lord Grey and presented to the winning team.

be helpful would be occasional correspondence and a lunch once or twice a year in which he could open up over a broad range of subjects.[112]

December 13, 1968

Dear Dr. McLuhan,

I would like to thank you very much for your letter of December 2nd. As always, I read with great interest your comments. I would also like to say how very grateful I am for your kind offer of help.

Given the difficulty that both of us have with schedules, it would be most helpful to me if, as in the past, you could take the trouble to send me from time to time your comments and suggestions. I also feel sure that there will be occasions when we can get together and talk more fully about matters of common interest. Perhaps lunch or dinner, from time to time?

I do appreciate very much the interest that you have displayed on my behalf by your letters and I value the ideas that they contain. I hope that I will benefit from your continued interest and thinking.

Yours sincerely,
Pierre E. Trudeau
With all good wishes for Christmas and the New Year.

112 Handwritten notations from both the PM and Marc Lalonde agreeing to this suggestion.

1969

January 24, 1969

Dear Mr. Prime Minister:

Your very cool dealings with our very hot medium the press, naturally produces intense interface or friction. The press has to have hot quotes and sharp points of view. Real news is bad news. Since the press lives on advertising, and all advertising is good news, it takes a lot of bad news to sell all this good news. Even the good news of the gospel can only be sold by hellfire. Vatican II made a very big mistake in this matter as in other matters.

The comment about cool dealings with a very hot medium was likely prompted by press reaction to Trudeau's behaviour in London during the Commonwealth Conference earlier that month when, after one formal banquet, he slid down a banister.

The very cool corporate mask that is your major political asset goes naturally with processing of problems in dialogue rather than in the production of packaged answers. That is why I urge you to go on the air with small groups and to trade problems with them rather than seeking answers or stating mere points of view.

In his new book 'The Age of Discontinuity' (Harper & Row, 1969), my friend Peter Drucker presents a magnificent inventory of problems in current decision making. He hasn't a clue as to why these problems have arisen but he cries out for a new theory of organization. He indicates that every organization in the world whether in the home or the school, the business or the political or the religious, has broken down today regardless of ideology or geography. On page 223 he focuses these problems onto the concept of the new 'ministate'. Every centralist organization large or small is now broken up into mini-states; even the

Catholic individual, as he relates to the Mystical Body, regards himself as a mini-state.

This is the exact antithesis of 16th century individualism based on a private interpretation of scripture. Superficially, doctrinal anarchy today and 16th century schismaticism look alike. Strict regard to structural character enables one to avoid confusion.

The change in all organization today is the result of putting fast electric information services around slow ones. Jet City transforms the globe into a single metropolis but it also destroys all existing metropolitan areas based on slow transport. In the same way, the telephone destroys the bureaucracy based on the memo or the letter.

Paradoxically, the slow system is 'open' and the fast one is 'closed'. Electric telecommunications create multitudes of tribally structured mini-states. These now begin to appear inside all the older maxi-states whether of business or politics. The unions and universities are mini-states, so are the police, the armed services, all media and all branches of business and government bureaucracies. The hierarchy of the organization chart is finished. Job specialism leads to role-playing in the global theatre.

You are the only political image of our time able to use the T.V. medium without being forced to become a tribal buffoon or cartoon like De Gaulle.[113] All the other political figures of the Western world are merely faded photographs on the T.V. medium.[114]

F.D.R.[115] had the press against him and this was his major asset as long as he relied on radio. But radio is a hot medium and fostered the lecture. T.V. permits audience participation in problem sharing. T.V. is a mini-state that has created various other ones such as the teeny-boppers and the hippies to say nothing of innumerable separatist tribes around the globe.

Most cordial good wishes,
Marshall McLuhan

---

113 Charles de Gaulle, president of France from 1959 to 1969.

114 This paragraph was marked out on the left margin by a vertical line, added by the reader, possibly Trudeau (the original is stamped as having been seen by the prime minister).

115 Franklin Delano Roosevelt, president of the United States from 1933 to 1945.

February 13, 1969

MEMORANDUM FOR THE PRIME MINISTER

From: J. M. Davey

Re: Letter from Dr. Marshall McLuhan

I am attaching a possible reply to Dr. McLuhan's letter suggesting that he give some thought to the use of television in association with such conferences as the one on constitutional matters.[116]

I recommend that you take a moment to study Dr. McLuhan's letter, particularly paragraphs marked 1 and 2 on page 2.

I spent about 30 hours watching the television and listening to commentaries during the three days of the conference and, while I was very happy indeed with the way in which it proceeded and the education that it provided to the viewers, nevertheless there was something about the process that was disturbing me which I was unable to define. I think the answer lies in Dr. McLuhan's letter. In essence, we put a fast electric information service, namely television, around a slow one, which is the deliberative process involved when a committee studies a subject.

In effect, we short-circuited the provincial representatives by letting electors participate in the process. After having heard the evidence provided by the speakers and by the commentators on the various issues, the electors were ready to cast their mental votes but there was no opportunity. Matters were sent off for further study by committee.

This had the same anti-climactic effect of a magazine serial, when at the high point of the drama, the action is interrupted with the statement "See next week's exciting installment to find out what happens".

I believe this explains the underlying impatience of the reporters who were concerned, in their questions to you, that no hard results had been achieved and everything is now going to committees.

116 In Ottawa, from February 10 to 12, there had been a First Ministers conference on constitutional review.

I seriously believe that we will have to rethink our approach[117] to constitutional change or at least the way in which we use television in the process. Perhaps Dr. McLuhan would have some ideas and it could be extremely valuable and fascinating for us to explore this subject with him.

February 13, 1969.

Dear Dr. McLuhan:

Thank you very much indeed for your letter of January 24th. Because of the preparations for the Constitutional Conference, I did not have the opportunity to read it until today. On reflection, I feel this was rather fortunate, for now that the conference is over, a number of the ideas have acquired a particular significance.

If you could take the time, I would be more than interested to have your views on the impact of television on conferences such as these. It does look as if there will be others in the future and I would like to see how we could use such occasions to help Canadians to better appreciate their country and the problems of its government.

Perhaps, if you are coming to Ottawa in the next month or so, we could have lunch or dinner together or, alternatively, I could send a member of my staff, Mr. Jim Davey, to see you in Toronto at your convenience.

Again, my thanks for your very valued comments and suggestions.

Yours sincerely,
[P.E.T.]

117 The words "rethink our approach" were underlined by Trudeau, who also wrote "Good Point" in the margin. A memo from Mary E. Macdonald, Trudeau's secretary, draws Davey's attention to this comment.

March 12, 1969[118]

Dear Mr. Prime Minister:

It isn't feasible for me to be in Ottawa during the next month since I am racing to meet a deadline with a new book. However, it would be possible for me to chat with Mr. Jim Davey here.

It would be helpful if he had some acquaintance with my written things. That would save time that would otherwise be spent in capsulating. At least, Mr. Davey could familiarize me with what seemed to you to be the "crunch in current political hang-ups."

Cordially,
Marshall McLuhan

March 31, 1969

MEMORANDUM FOR MR. LALONDE

From: J. M. Davey

Re: Toronto Visit – Thursday, April 3rd

I will be in Toronto next Thursday to visit Dr. Marshall McLuhan. This is a follow-up from an exchange of correspondence between Dr. McLuhan and the Prime Minister. I want to discuss the whole question of the use of television as a vehicle of public information but with particular emphasis on such events as Federal-Provincial Conferences.

While I am there I also intend to meet Superintendent Harold Genno, of the Metropolitan Police. I gather, from the attached clipping,

118 This letter was preceded by a February 17, 1969, request to Trudeau from A.C. Spectorsky, editorial director of *Playboy*, inviting him to comment in their letters section on their McLuhan interview in the March 1969 issue. It was marked "No answer" (underlined twice) by press secretary Roméo LeBlanc. In that interview, the claim is made that "Canada's turned-on Prime Minister Pierre Trudeau engages [McLuhan] in monthly bull sessions designed to improve his television image," but the correspondence I have seen doesn't support this. Eric McLuhan and Zingrone, eds., *Essential McLuhan*, 233.

that he has made a study of the question of police tactics and relations during public manifestations. Don Wall[119] is aware of my visit.

While we are on the subject, you might want to consider asking a number of questions of the Department of National Defense. Last week the Government was in the position where it might have had to furnish armed forces to assist the Montreal police. In this instance, the Government would have had no option had a written request been made for such support. While everyone concerned is happy that the eventuality did not arise, I can't help asking myself what would have been the outcome if it had.

Question:

1) If the Armed Forces are under this obligation, what in their training would give them the necessary experience and competence?
2) Do the Armed Forces receive specialized training in crowd control and relations with manifesters under such conditions?
3) Which troops would have been used on this occasion, were they in particular, adequately trained to carry out the task?
4) What will we do in future if we receive another such request?

April 14, 1969

Dear Mr. Prime Minister:

Thank you for sending Mr. Jim Davey. We had a very pleasant chat. Please let me clarify at once that matter of consulting fees. Naturally it would not concern any personal conversation between us, whether in private or by phone.

As for "remuneration" for consulting with your colleagues on a variety of problems, it might be possible to arrange fellowships for people

119 Based on a number of online references (such as *Last Stop, Paris: The Assassination of Mario Bachand and the Death of the FLQ*, by Michael McLoughlin, https://books.google.com), I believe that Wall was involved in security matters, including serving as assistant secretary for security and intelligence in the Privy Council Office.

of your own choice to study at the Centre for a few weeks. This, in turn, may call for some resource material to assist them.

For example, Paul Hellyer's report[120] is entirely a 19th-century study of "hardware" that omits all awareness of the new dominance of the knowledge industries. As electronic "software", or information, creates the main environment or garb-age of the planet and cities, the meanings and role of buildings and industries are completely altered. In the knowledge industries a man can work at home, or beside his home, as readily as "downtown." Business itself has become a dozen times more involved in education than schools and colleges. The educational budgets of personnel on company time (not even mentioning the armed services) is twenty times that of the communal budget for schools and colleges. This new dominance of information and the knowledge industries completely alters what has been called "zoning." Nineteenth-century hardware industry is now receding into insignificance. This means the end of the old division between work and residence.

Jet city is a circulating city. People now circulate in the same way that books used to, one hundred years ago. This means that it is pure folly to spend money on classrooms for schools and colleges. It is much cheaper and more effective to send the young to the areas of the world in which they have need to immerse for their studies. This is "crash-programming" instead of the assembly-line package job they now get. But Dr. Bissell[121] has asked, "What will I do with all these buildings?" The answer is simple. They will now serve for continued education of the elders of the tribe.

As knowledge replaces experience in human affairs, senior business men feel a deep urge to go back to the campus. Having circulated around the world, and having immersed themselves in many problems, they now feel the need to specialize. That is, they are eager to do what the young detest, and the young are eager to do what the elders are fed up with. These inversions, or reversals, result from the exhaustion of the potential of any form, as Aristotle points out in The Physics. It is a pattern of growth: as the caterpillar said as he scornfully watched

120 In January, the Task Force on Housing and Urban Development, headed by Hellyer, issued its report, which was not accepted by the Trudeau cabinet. Hellyer resigned from the cabinet the same month this letter was written.

121 Claude Bissell, president of the University of Toronto from 1958 to 1971.

the flutterings of a butterfly: "You'll never catch me up in one of those danged things!" It is also known as the Hertz law: the consequences of the images will be the images of the consequences.

McLuhan's language, in these letters and elsewhere, and his often corny jokes, can be jarring to sensitive contemporary ears and might have been considered in poor taste at the time of writing – "coloured" here, in the age of the Black Power movement, or "paraplegic soccer game" (June 3, 1968) or the references to "Women's Lib," even though not used in a negative way. In his February 24, 1977, letter, he apologizes for any suggestion he insulted Trudeau in an interview by suggesting he has a hint in his face of "the native Indian... the Red man." I don't know what prejudices McLuhan held, but I think these examples simply reflect what we too charitably refer to as the language of a man of his times.

The big TV networks, including the C.B.C., are collapsing by attempting packaged programming, 19th century style. For the same reasons the same fate is overtaking the bureaucracies and governments of the world. It is the attempt to pursue goals and policies in an instantaneous world of total public involvement.

Last Sunday, after the Smothers Brothers show,[122] the C.B.C. did a study on "violence." It consisted in simply asking a diverse group in age and occupation what they thought violence was. They did not ask about any cures[123] for violence. There was instant and total participation. Let me take the opportunity of this instance to urge you to experiment in problem inventories with small diversified groups. It is important to avoid all attempt at solutions. The "solution" is always the mark of the 19th century packaging mind. The real solution is in the problem itself, as in any detective story.

Jacques Ellul has written a new book entitled Political Illusions. Under existing political forms, he says, the first illusion is participation. The second illusion is that there are solutions, e.g. there is no ignorance where there is no learning. There is no poverty where there is no affluence. There is no privacy where there is no public. These, and many forms, are complementary. The white man creates the coloured man,

122 The *Smothers Brothers Comedy Hour*, which ran on CBS from 1967 to 1969, was often both funny and politically controversial.

123 Someone underlined this in red.

as affluence creates poverty. A convict has no privacy. He has solitude. A tribal man has no privacy. Under electric conditions there can be no privacy. The privacy invaders are the bulwark of the new knowledge industries, from the pollsters, to the insurance companies, and the credit ratings, "the eye in the sky", the age of the "snoop."

I collect funny stories since they are infallible indexes of public grievance. You cannot only predict, but pin-point areas of grievance by the jokes that circulate. There are now floods of bi-lingual jokes, as well as Newfie jokes.[124] Perhaps you have heard of the big Newfie break-through: the first hernia transplant!... etc. The reason for the flood of Newfie jokes is quite simply the shift of the Newfoundland population from rural to urban areas. There is a new interface, creating much irritation. East Berliners express their grievances by pointing to the great Russian breakthrough: the crossing of glow-worms with body lice now permits the entire population of Russia to read Pravda[125] in bed at night!

Our own grievances concerning drugs and cops may break out in many forms, e.g. the reporter checking the man-in-the-street opinions on LSD, is told: "I think he is a great President, even if he has many enemies. History will vindicate him!" He then asks, "What about marijuana?" He is told, "Well, my wife and I spent a week there last year and found it absolutely delightful!" In a quite different category, Lord Birkenhead asked, jocularly, to render a legal opinion on whiskey and water, observed: "Making water in public is a misdemeanor; making whiskey in private is a felony." Woodrow Wilson,[126] asked how many times he thought it permissible to use the same speech, replied: "I can't answer that question, I'm still using mine!"

I hope you find some of this useful.

Sincere good wishes,
[M.M.]

---

124 In pre-politically correct times, Newfie jokes were the English Canadian equivalent of jokes in other cultures that single out one particular group as being less intelligent than the majority and turn its members into the butt of bad jokes.

125 *Pravda*, a daily newspaper at the time, was the official propaganda organ of the Soviet government. I think McLuhan's use of "Russia" here was its common usage during the Soviet era, using "Russia" to refer to the U.S.S.R. of which it was only a part, albeit the most important part.

126 Woodrow Wilson, president of the United States from 1913 to 1921.

April 23, 1969

MEMORANDUM FOR MR. LALONDE

From: J. M. Davey

Re: Marshall McLuhan

I am attaching a copy of a letter from Dr. McLuhan which he wrote since my recent visit with him.

My recommendation is that he be invited for an evening with the Prime Minister, in Ottawa, so that he could spell out his ideas of what could be done in the field of communications. Such a meeting should be very small and probably not include anyone other than the Prime Minister, Dr. McLuhan and yourself.

I believe Dr. McLuhan can be a source of valuable insights but, because he is a somewhat overpowering personality, the problem will be to find if any arrangements with him can be effective, and, if so, which.

May 29, 1969

Dear Mr. Prime Minister:

The enclosed tam is an official Maple Leaf tartan designed and made here in Toronto and registered with the proper Scottish tartan buffs of Edinburgh, Scotland! I was thrilled to discover that there is a Maple Leaf tartan of great attractiveness. I am presently having a blazer made of it and the material is supplied by Mr. Richardson, Richardson's Blazers, 546 Yonge St.

I am sure there is lots of Scottish blood in your ancestry. The fur-traders, who are mostly Scots, intermarried with the French very freely.

I like to think of you in a proper Maple Leaf tartan kilt!

Most cordially,
Marshall McLuhan

P.S. The kilt, of course, is a mini-skirt, such as is worn by all tribal peoples. The mini-skirt is the same for men and women. Sex is not taken seriously by corporate societies. Hence the seeming nonsense of the hippies in this area.

P.P.S. A joke that may serve your turn: the witness in the stand was asked by the judge: "Did you really see him bite off the man's ear?" Answer: "No, I did not." Question: "Then why in blazes are you here in the witness stand?" Answer: "I saw him spit the ear out!"

The Distant Early Warning (DEW) Line was a predominantly Arctic line of radar and other tracking stations built by the U.S. and operated by Canadians as a joint security project, beginning in the mid-1950s. McLuhan used DEW-LINE as the name of a short-lived newsletter he produced at this time to warn of the influences of new media and technologies.

While attending the idiotic Bilderbung Conference on world unrest I spoke to George Ball[127] of the U.S. I said: "The Canadians are a very cool crowd." He replied: "Not according to my mail." I asked him: "What was the cause for irritation?" He then explained his plan for taking over Canada. I replied: "Well, Mr. Ball, to be quite frank, I have not only never heard of your plan, but I have never heard of <u>you</u> before in my life. Why don't you all come up and live on the Dew Line which you have built? All Americans could live up there without even being noticed!"

Later he told me the story about George Jessup[128] [sic] and Dean Atchison [sic][129]. Atchison was complaining about his long, sleepless nights and Jessop [sic] said: "Try these, Dean." Later that night, about 3:00 a.m., he had a frantic call from Dean Atchison. "George, I can't swallow these damned things you gave me!" To which George replied: "Dean, those are ear plugs!"

I hope you have already begun to entertain yourself by paging through the hilarious book about bureaucracy by Laurence Peter, <u>The</u>

127 George Ball who, at the time of this meeting, was about to begin three months serving as US ambassador to the United Nations.

128 I assume McLuhan did not mean George Jessel, a popular comic at the time, but US diplomat and international jurist Philip Jessup (1897–1986).

129 Dean Acheson, statesman and presidential advisor.

Peter Principle (Wm. Morrow & Co., N.Y., 1969). The Peter Principle is stated in a word or two on page 25: "In a hierarchy every employee tends to rise to his level of incompetence." The corollary is on page 27: "In time, every post tends to be occupied by an employee who is incompetent to carry out its duties." This constitutes the normal state of equilibrium in all organizations. One might re-word Lord Acton to say: absolute powerlessness corrupts absolutely.

M.M.

June 18, 1969.

Dear Mr. McLuhan:

Many thanks for the Maple Leaf tartan tam. Some people in Sherbrooke[130] would perhaps have liked to see it on June 24th!

With warm regards and wishes,
Yours sincerely,
P. E. Trudeau

July 3, 1969

MEMORANDUM FOR THE PRIME MINISTER

From: J. M. Davey

Re: Sussex Dinner with Dr. Marshall McLuhan, July 9th.

Dr. McLuhan was very happy to accept your invitation for dinner next Wednesday.

McLuhan is essentially a monologist and requires very little priming to encourage a discourse. He does feel much happier in a smaller group and my suggestion would be that you invite no more than about two or three other guests.

130 This refers to the riot that broke out on Sherbrooke St. in Montreal in Trudeau's presence on June 24, 1968.

You might want to choose from amongst the following:

Marc Lalonde
Fernand Cadieux[131]
Romeo LeBlanc[132]
Ivan Head[133]
Gordon Gibson

You may wish me to attend, but I do not personally regard my presence as essential.

July 8, 1969

MEMORANDUM FOR THE PRIME MINISTER

From: J. M. Davey

Re: Sussex Dinner with Dr. Marshall McLuhan

Messrs. Jamieson,[134] Head and Wylie[135] are most pleased to accept the invitation to dine with Dr. McLuhan and yourself tomorrow night at 24 Sussex. I have informed each of your guests that dinner would likely last from 7:30 until 9:30 as you have another engagement later in the evening.[136]

I will meet Dr. McLuhan earlier in the day and arrange that he will be at Sussex by 7:30. Ivan Head will arrange to look after Dr. McLuhan at the conclusion of the evening.

---

131 Cadieux was an intellectual inspiration to Trudeau and others in his circle as young adults and, until his death in 1976, served as special advisor to the prime minister.

132 Press secretary Roméo LeBlanc became a politician and, eventually, governor general of Canada. His son, Dominic LeBlanc, is a close friend of Prime Minister Justin Trudeau, in whose cabinet he serves.

133 Ivan Head, a foreign policy specialist who was part of Trudeau's inner circle of advisors, "was the inspiration for Trudeau's decision to develop a network of personal friendships with Third World leaders, and to become an authority on north-south relations." Gwyn, *Northern Magus*, 83.

134 Politician and diplomat Donald Jamieson was a member of Trudeau's cabinet.

135 Liberal Party operative Torrance Wylie.

136 Richard Gwyn and others note that Trudeau always stopped work at 9:30 p.m. to prepare for the next day.

I have briefed each of your guests on the background to the dinner and the likely form that it would take, i.e., more of a discourse by Dr. McLuhan than a dialogue.

Dr. McLuhan will very likely broach with you the desirability of yourself appearing on television in conversations with different groups of the population to discuss problems of the country. You may wish to probe him somewhat on the value of such an exercise.

Other subjects where I believe Dr. McLuhan's insights are very interesting include:

Youth
Education
Organizations (particularly government).

J. M. Davey

July 17, 1969

Dear Jim:

The visit with Trudeau was most delightful. For now, just a note on some of the economic and executive patterns that Barry Nevitt and I are working with in our book. One of these may have immediate relevancy.

As you know, in airplane controls, when you go through the sound barrier the control patterns reverse. You push the stick forward when you wish to ascend and vice versa. The same applies in economic controls, and under electronic conditions of speed. Rasminsky[137] still assumes the pre-electronic speeds of slow movement. The older economists including Keynes[138] had no awareness of this reversal pattern at speedup points. When going into any of the variables or details of wages and prices, the mere matter of interest rates is the obvious control stick in question. By pushing up on the interest stick the "plane" is going to make a very sudden descent. By pulling up on the stick or pushing up interest rates the effect will be the exact opposite of the one intended.

137 Louis Rasminsky, Governor of the Bank of Canada from 1961 to 1973.

138 John Maynard Keynes (1883–1946), influential British economist.

This reversal principle works in every field of decision making whatever. The fast environmental spin destroys the slower environmental structure just as the plane destroys rail or telephone destroys postal and memo systems and the organization chart.

I have had much yardage out of your joke about the man with both feet planted firmly on the ground. Had you heard the synonym for the "Pill" – Absorbine Jr.?

Cordially,[139]
[M.M.]

August 27, 1969

Dear Jim:

Working to complete The Executive as Dropout: The Future of Management. Have had much occasion to consider inflation in relation to general social speed-up. Am sure money has little to do with inflation. Of course, a penny at computer speeds could serve to affect all the transactions of the total currency. The mistake is to isolate money from our economy when most of the information transactions are no longer monetary. Anthropologists are very conscious of the incongruity of studying sex in non-Western societies (it would be ridiculous to study the economic life of the Navaho!). Sex only isolated out in recent times in the West and is now merging once more with the total culture. Real inflation is caused by speed-up in the total society.

In the 1920s it was the advent of radio that put a new rim-spin on the whole show, including the sound track on film toward the end of the decade. I saw my first talkie in 1929. It was The Coconuts with the Marx Bros.[140] An example of speed-up and inflation is summer school in the university. The entire planet is given an extra spin, a third term. Having taught summer school for several years in the States, I know

139 There are many handwritten notations at the top of this letter, which appear to involve wordplay, some of it McLuhan-inspired. I assume Davey was the author.

140 The film was actually titled *The Cocoanuts*. The Marx Brothers were internationally famous US entertainers in several media during the first half of the 20th century.

the results. As compared with the two semester Canadian school, with its long summer (practically a sabbatical), there is, in the American tri-semester patterns, gradual loss of dialogue both among students and faculty, and a great increase in bureaucratic activity. Summer school keeps American universities "in the black".

Our current inflation is computer inspired, with TV playing a major role in shifting real war into a clash of iconics and corporate images. "Hardware" war (the military industrial complex) is obsolete. Even atomic warfare has been by-passed by "softer" and more penetrating weapons, whether of gas or information.

A second glance at "money" reveals that it has shifted steadily from bullion (hardware) to credit (software).

Best wishes for a reposeful summer,
[M.M.]

There is now a large gap in the correspondence. This was the period during which Trudeau was falling in love with Margaret Sinclair, while dealing with the usual affairs of state and, perhaps above all, the developing FLQ (Front de Libération du Québec) situation that would culminate in the 1970 October Crisis. When the correspondence picks up again, McLuhan uses as his starting point a recent viewing of the 1969 political thriller *Z*, in which a right-wing government attacks pacifists supporting the opposition.

1970

March 2, 1970

Dear Jim:

A couple of basic principles apropos administrative dynamics popped into mind while watching the movie "Z". In a word, any conventional bureaucracy becomes a police state when speeded up by a new technology such as telephone or telex. Just as Machiavelli[141] could regard the state as a work of art as soon as the medieval order had been scrapped by the new speed-up of Gutenberg[142] technology, so our political structures become "works of art" as they are scrapped by new technology. The movie has become a work of art since TV. The planet has become a work of art since the satellite, i.e. the planet in the sense of "Nature" has been scrapped and we now confront it as an art project in the name of "pollution." Once surrounded by human artefacts, Nature is a mess. A good example of new technology turning bureaucracy into a police state is the traffic question. As the motor car becomes obsolete and traffic is aided by helicopters and computers, etc. you have the extreme instance of police state resulting from the speed-up of obsolete technology.

The second theme. Drugs. The clue is in prohibition of the '20s. Booze was not new. It was the panic that was new. So with drugs today. It is the panic that is new. The new radio environment of the '20s created a new primitivism and tribalism which we associate with the jazz age. Tribal people cannot abide booze. It sends them berserk. They are already excessively involved in each other without stimulants. The

141 Niccolo Machiavelli (1469–1527), Italian philosopher and political mastermind.

142 Johannes Gutenberg (1398–1468) introduced movable type printing into Europe, ushering in the print revolution and the world of mass communications.

WASP,[143] on the other hand, needs gallons of booze in order to be sociable. In the '20s the WASP had gone tribal and booze began to terrify him.

The key to the drug panic is TV. TV intensifies the already numerous forms of inner-tripping. Colour TV is a psychedelic input. The kids are simply putting jam on jam when they take to drugs. They seem to imagine that it helps them to relate to an electric speed world, whereas they are quite unable to relate to the fractured and fragments specialties of a pre-electric school and goal and job system.

In the '20s booze created a huge police state as we tried to prop up the old form of social arrangements. Drugs likewise provide a field-day for the Mafia as we try to maintain the patterns of the pre-electric age while the kids are miming electric speeds and the externalization of their nervous systems created by electric circuitry.

The third matter concerns the need for a program on "learned ignorance". What has often been called "trained incapacity" flourishes as never before in our bureaucratic society. Computer speeds actually are making practical the return to the "cottage economy". It may soon be fashionable to run a factory from the kitchen. The Middle Ages have returned to us long ago by electric means as you can see in the kids' costumes and in their avid pursuit of role-playing. With the satellite surround the planet becomes a global theatre with the audience as actor. Hence the new politics of "unrest". The public has no intention of remaining in the spectator role. Hence a program in which all the hang-ups of the learned in the arts and sciences and in all areas of our Establishment would be one means of getting the audience directly into the administrative act. Again, the pattern of the program should be inventory of hang-ups, not solutions. If the audience makes instant breakthroughs on previously insoluble matters, fine. This would happen, but it needn't be the main purpose of the program.

Cordial regards,
[M.M.]

143 This acronym, which started to become popular in North America in the 1950s, means "white Anglo-Saxon Protestant."

June 18, 1970

Dear Jim:

This came like an electric bolt from the blue for a nut – the nut being me! If you start with the last few lines on pages 17 and 18 [of Krugman[144]], then look at the bottom of page 13, you will know what you are in for. Krugman has validated quantitatively everything I have been saying, even though he doesn't understand very much about it. The evidence that <u>all</u> media communicate themselves by transforming the participant but fail to convey very much of their supposed "content" applies as much to English or Russian as to print or telephone or TV. It throws a flash of awareness into the mystery of the blocks in the so-called teaching and learning processes.

People have always been able to absorb the media, whether linguistic or material. Their performance in this area is super-human compared to their power to absorb "content". The ability of a child to learn a complex mother tongue by three is a fantastic feat never duplicated again by any other activity of the individual human life. Suzuki's[145] discovery of "learning by immersion" is really the transfer of the learning effort to the media rather than to their content. The implications in politics are as weird as for education and commerce. When I gave a talk in Montreal yesterday to the Association of Industrial Advertisers, the General Electric report findings created a considerable hush and were duly omitted from the press reports.

Just wanted you to have an early look at this for the benefit of your department as well.

[M.M.]

144 Public opinion researcher Herbert E. Krugman, manager of corporate public opinion at the General Electric Company from 1967 to 1983. McLuhan is citing the GE report mentioned later in the letter.

145 Shinichi Suzuki (1898–1998), Japanese musician and educator.

December 3, 1970

Dear Mr. Trudeau:

Since the dinner on Friday, November 27, much of the time I have been down with flu. My first act since recovery is to thank you for the wonderful evening and the incomparable honour which you conferred upon me and my family. Teri[146] and Corinne insist that their lives have an entirely new dimension as a result of that event! Part of the satisfaction, however, was in the assured feeling that each of us was in fact being entirely "himself". The events of the next day – the unveiling of the dramatic hat and cloak, the kick-off, and the Alouette triumph[147] – all seemed to be an extended part of the same euphoric experience of our dinner meeting.

Your comments on the political developments in Canada have been recurring in my thoughts. I know some good fruit will come of this, and I shall report to you before too long.

In friendship and esteem,
[M.M.]

December 11, 1970

Dear Mr. McLuhan:

I was pleased and touched at your kindness in sending to me the inscribed copies of "Culture Is Our Business", "From Cliché to Archetype", and "The Literary Criticism of Marshall McLuhan 1943/1962".

I will be delighted to have them in my own personal library, not only so that I can have them close at hand but also because they will be a pleasant reminder of an enjoyable evening that I spent in company with Mrs. McLuhan, Teri, yourself, and the Daveys.

It was very thoughtful indeed of you to think of me in this way.

Yours sincerely,
Pierre E. T.

146 Teresa McLuhan (b.1945) and her twin sister, Mary, are the second-born of McLuhan's six children.

147 The Montreal Alouettes football team defeated the Calgary Stampeders 23 to 10 in Toronto to win the Grey Cup.

1971

March 5, 1971

Dear Pierre:

We rejoice in your marriage and in the enormous discomfiture of many of your enemies! We also rejoice in the loveliness of your bride, and in sharing the Catholic faith with both of us.[148]

Many blessings.
[M.M.]

March 8, 1971

Dear Jim:

We have naturally been delighted by the great Pierre and Margaret wedding event. Surely there is nothing in the history of democratic politics to match the mise en scène of this event. It was not only a personal but a political triumph, putting both the opposition and the media in Pierre's pocket, as it were. The media people have to be grateful for being duped, since their unpreparedness was very much part of the show.

In this very connection I have a new essay, a copy of which I am enclosing, explaining that, why, and how the user is the content of any medium or environment. I am still working on the many features of this situation, and am quite at a loss to explain why I had been unable to see so obvious a fact before. When Trudeau "uses" the media, as in the current nuptial drama, he is their content. When they use him, they are the content. It is a sort of reciprocal hi-jacking. Only yesterday I was

148 The day before, Trudeau had married Margaret Joan Sinclair, almost 30 years his junior, taking the country by surprise, as even their relationship had been kept hidden from the media.

reading a chapter on "Judgment and Truth in Aquinas"[149] by my friend, Fr. Owens,[150] here at the Medieval Institute.[151] He concludes: "They involve the traditional Aristotelian view that the cognitive agent itself becomes and is the thing known… Its structure comes from the thing known, and not from any a priori in the intellect."

It turns out then, that my communication theory is Thomistic to the core. It has the further advantage of being able to explain Aquinas and Aristotle in modern terms. We are the content of anything we use, if only because these things are extensions of ourselves. The meaning of the pencil, or the chair I use is the interplay between me and these things. Again, the message of these things is the sum of the changes that result from their social use. Thus, I have added two features to "the medium is the message", namely the content and the meaning, Perhaps Pierre Juneau[152] or someone at C.R.T.C. would like to have this essay apropos the problem of "Canadian content"? The consequence for the discussion of the problem of Canadian content for the media is drastically simplified by noticing that the user is the content. If Canadians use or

The struggle over Canadian content – whether government should be allowed to control it, what the proper amounts might be, even how to define it – has never gone away. In the early days of government control of the issue, which includes the time of my grade 12 project, "The Media Make the Message," I was told by Jim Rennie, then the entertainment editor at the *Toronto Star*, that "We cover Canadian talent more out of nationalism and obligation than talent or the belief it will be read."

Jean Wright, then managing editor of *Chatelaine* magazine, was even harsher, telling me that "You can't say to people that part of their duty is to sit down and read a dull article about a dull person that you don't want to read about" with the only exceptions in Canada being "Nancy Greene, Pierre Berton, Gordon Sinclair, Betty Kennedy, Leonard Cohen, Monique Leyrac maybe, Pierre Trudeau – who else is there?"

149 Saint Thomas Aquinas (1225–1274).

150 Joseph Owens, scholar of medieval philosophy.

151 Pontifical Institute of Mediaeval Studies at the University of Toronto.

152 Pierre Juneau, first chairman of the Canadian Radio-television and Telecommunications Commission, established in 1968.

watch American programs or drive American cars, it is the Canadians who are the content of these things. The meaning is in the resulting interplay or dialogue between Canadians and these things, but there can be no question that the Canadian user of American things is the content of these things. The meaning and the message are something else. It is unfortunate that the C.R.T.C. ever involved itself in the question of content, especially since it does not understand the nature of media at all, except as hardware.

A note on hi-jacking apropos media and politics: in our book The Executive as Dropout, which is close to being sent to the publisher, we have a section on the nature of hi-jacking in business and in politics. Realizing that the very nature of hi-jacking is related to new services and environments, I asked a New York tycoon whether there were any parallels to hi-jacking in business. He replied at once that the bigger the business, the easier it is to hi-jack it. He said the biggest banks in the world today are being sued by their own shareholders for misallocation of funds. The Penn Central[153] discovered that its entire funds had been appropriated for non-transportation uses. This is done in the bookkeeping division of the firm, unbeknown to the rest of the operation. It is almost impossible to check. Hence the larger the operation, the less it knows about whether it is going "to land". Cities are hi-jacked every day by developers who simply pressure the bureaucracy into "landing" in areas favourable to the developers. Countries can be hi-jacked as readily as a big business.

It is a useful metaphor since it really concerns the problems of the new service environments as created by jet planes at high speed. The question arises whether the passengers could agree to be hi-jacked by democratic process. Could everybody on the plane agree to go to Cuba instead of Miami? This raises the problem of swinging blocks of votes as a form of hi-jacking. Historically, the creation of the C.P.R.[154] could be considered under the aspect of hi-jacking the country. Pollution is another form of taking over of an entire service environment, whether of land, water, or air and perverting its uses. If some private enterprise in

153 The Penn Central Transportation Company which, in 1970, filed for bankruptcy, at that point the largest bankruptcy in US history.

154 Canadian Pacific Railway, Canada's first transcontinental railway, completed in 1885.

fact uses land, water, or air, it is that enterprise that becomes the content of the environment in question, just as the hold-up man on the plane, by assuming the use of the plane to himself, becomes the content of the plane by usurping the role of all the other passengers.

Since the user as content is not a figure of speech but a basic dynamic and cognitative relationship, I think you will find that it can be pushed all the way as a means of orientation in media, economics and politics. I suggest that it can be the basis for a complete restatement of political and economic realities in the information age of the wired planet.

Cordial greetings,
yrs
Marshall

March 24, 1971.

Dear Marshall and Corinne:[155]

My wife and I were delighted to receive your message. It was most thoughtful of you. Both of us want to say thank you.

Very sincerely,
Pierre E.T.

During this next significant gap in their correspondence, McLuhan had a serious illness from which he never fully recovered, and Trudeau was dealing with national issues including inflation, unemployment and the failure of the Victoria Conference in British Columbia. Victoria was the culminating event in a series of conferences representing Trudeau's first formal attempt to patriate the Canadian constitution, although, as he notes in *Memoirs*, attempts had been made by others as early as 1927.

155 First example of Trudeau addressing the McLuhans by their given names. Interestingly, he does not then go on to use his own wife's given name.

September 21, 1971

Dear Mr. Trudeau:

In the violent seas of "news" and publicity in which you have had to exist in recent months, I have refrained from saying anything whatever. I want you to know that you are in my prayers and that I have been perpetually amazed at the imaginative skill with which you have managed the utterly conflicting jobs with which you are confronted. You are immeasurably the greatest Prime Minister Canada has ever had, the first who has ever been equipped with an awareness of contemporary culture. Heath[156] and Nixon are provincial schoolboys beside you. With this advantage of your pre-eminence and contemporaneity is the backlash of uncomprehending fury and envy which they elicit. Your detractors cannot imagine how humble one is made by the recognition of the scope of your problems.

Some while ago I sent Jim Davey a manuscript of my Executive as Dropout which I have written with Barrington Nevitt. He is an electric engineer and a management consultant with long experience in Europe and South American countries. Our book is now in the press and will, I hope, be of direct aid in relating decision-making to the new fact of speed-up.

Corinne and I rejoice in your marriage and keep you and Margaret in our prayers.

In a few days our daughter, Teri, has a new book on the orations of American Indian chiefs to their tribes. It will be published in the U.S. and in Canada, and you will of course receive a copy. Teri hopes that it may have some direct use in focusing the matter of Indian and ethnic minorities. The alienated ones have a natural intuition of ecology, since they are the victims of its absence.

[M.M.]

156 Edward Heath, prime minister of Great Britain from 1970 to 1974.

September 29, 1971

Dear Jim:

Naturally, Nevitt and I are watching the changing relationship between Canada and the U.S. in relation to the analysis we did on hardware and software in our Executive as Dropout, which I think you have. It is now in the press for early Spring publication.

A great advantage which Canada enjoys over the U.S. is the relative absence of massive installations. We enjoy many of the 20th century opportunities of other "backward" countries. We are free to start in with the software and by-pass the hardware. That is our privilege for having missed the 19th century. Of course, areas like Montreal and Toronto, precisely to the degree to which they did have a 19th century are in a bad way. The message of the electric age is to by-pass these places also, and not to make their problems those of the country at large. Highly centralist hardware and hardware areas have to be regarded as bad investments that are better forgotten. Sooner or later the U.S. will have to write off its big cities and hardware also. In this situation the U.K. is almost helpless.

I want to ask your counsel and aid in some anti-abortion strategies which I am beginning to be associated with. The abortion mill closely resembles Buchenwald.[157] People directly engaged in it would risk their lives to save the life of a two-year-old child from a car or truck. What has happened is a complete collapse of community awareness via specialism of function. As long as an operation or process is divided into sufficiently small segments, nobody feels any responsibility for anything. Communal awareness has no chance to come into play. This was the mystery of Buchenwald and such camps. A few weeks ago I spoke with Germans and Austrians directly related to those events. They were pious Catholics, and I asked them how they could have permitted these things. Their answer was simply "We just did our bit and were unaware of the other bits." It is by this type of programming that we can calmly expect our highways to deliver a given number of dead per

157 Nazi concentration camp operating in Weimar, Germany, from 1937 to 1945.

day or week. The really devastating programming is the destruction of perception and sensitivity by the creation of vast environments far exceeding human scale. The King Kong fantasies are direct expressions of the feeling most people have in their environments which have become monsters. Yet, the best intentioned bureaucrats in all governments are busily engaged in creating bigger and blacker King Kongs every day of the week. Meantime, the kids are repudiating the society and fleeing to small communes. Of course, the effect of current unemployment will be to reconcile many of them once more to the environment as it is.

I don't know why McLuhan thought his request for anti-abortion strategies would be well received. Trudeau, though personally opposed to abortion as a sin, did not believe it to be a crime (English, *Just Watch Me*, 112). Asked about abortion at a meeting of his riding association that November, he replied, "I don't think that I can speak with great authority about this mainly because I am not a woman." (Trudeau, *Conversation with Canadians*, 37.)

Trudeau was also personally against birth control. (Margaret Trudeau, *Beyond Reason*, 55.)

Our anti-abortion group here at St. Mike's needs to discover ways of presenting films on national networks, if possible. These films don't have to have any pro or con slant, if they are permitted to show the actual process. If any practical program has begun anywhere that you know of, I would be happy to hear about it.

Hoping you have had a good summer, and that your family is in the best of shape,

Warm regards,
Marshall

October 1, 1971.

Dear Marshall:

Thank you very much for your recent letter. Jim Davey keeps me informed of your activities and sends me from time to time copies of your correspondence to him, but I was certainly very pleased to hear from you directly. I will also be looking forward to your new book, "Executive as Dropout".

I am very flattered by some of your comments about me and I am very touched by your thoughtfulness for Margaret and myself.

My best wishes to Mrs. McLuhan and yourself, and also to Teri on the publication of her book.

Yours sincerely,
Pierre

October 25, 1971.

Dear Marshall and Corinne:

Many thanks for your prayerful good wishes. It was indeed kind of both of you to think of my birthday.

Best personal regards,
Sincerely,
Pierre

Another big gap in correspondence, with not even a letter congratulating the Trudeaus on the Christmas birth of their first child, Justin. During this gap, Trudeau met with Nixon in Washington and Nixon paid a visit to Ottawa, despite a vow to "never set foot in Canada so long as Trudeau was leader." (English, *Just Watch Me*, 169.)

1972

June 12, 1972.

Dear Marshall:

I was delighted indeed to receive from Barry Nevitt and yourself a copy of your new book, "Take Today: The Executive as Dropout" inscribed for Margaret and myself.

My first glance at the book has been all too tantalizingly brief but just enough to savour at once the vigorous and obvious craft of fellow players. I am looking forward with pleasure and anticipation to the prospect of enjoying the full performance soon.

Would you please pass on my thanks and congratulations to Barry Nevitt.

On behalf of Margaret and myself, best personal wishes to Corinne, Teri, the other members of your family, and yourself.

Yours sincerely,
Pierre E. T.

August 2, 1972

The Rt. Hon.[158] P.E. Trudeau,
Prime Minister
House of Commons
Ottawa, Ontario.

Dear Pierre:

Politics and the media present a tireless set of variations these days. Some of these variations are noted in Take Today: The Executive as Dropout which I hope you will find a moment to look at from time to time. It is not that I covet your personal approval so much as the hope that it may be of some usefulness in your extremely arduous course.

Recently, in Dublin and Paris and Athens, friends urged me to set up "Centres for Understanding Media." They had in mind a kind of dialogue that could be maintained among several such places with the help of a Newsletter or periodical brochure into which they could put their current problems and discoveries concerning the interplay between media and the major institutions of our time. It might be a great help to have such a Centre in Quebec, for example. If Quebec could see its patterns and role in our twentieth

McLuhan was not suggesting physical centres be built, but that a means of communications, such as a newsletter, be created. One needs to remember again that this was pre-Internet. He also seemed to understand that there might already have been too many buildings dedicated to education and, certainly, that they would have to be repurposed, most effectively "for continued education of the elders of the tribe." (April 14, 1969)

This letter was acknowledged by an aide and briefly responded to by Trudeau, and I imagine McLuhan was disappointed. But the prime minister was in a tough political season, getting ready to call a fall election. That election was held on October 30, and the Liberals hung onto power with only a very slim minority mandate. Trudeau then made major changes in his cabinet and inner advisory team, trading "intellectuals" for those "more politically minded." Jim Davey was among the casualties, although he remained a friend and informal advisor. (Trudeau, *Memoirs*, 160.)

158 I am including this heading information because it is the first time I know of when McLuhan uses, properly, "Rt. Hon." instead of "Hon."

century against the ground of other countries facing the same separatist pressures under media impact, it might greatly relieve tension and play down the merely personal feelings.

I consider that Canada has become a world Utopia, as it were, by chance. Our unique situation seems to me to be that we are the only country in the world without an "identity." We have two identities which in effect polarize one another and create a very important pattern of complementarity. It is a complementarity of a special kind, deriving, on the one hand, from a great land power (France) and, on the other hand, a great sea power (England). Canada, in a most eminent way, embraces both of these cultural forms of land and sea. There is also the fact that English in this century has become a world language through the particular agency of jazz and rock. Yet the French tongue richly modifies and controls this enormous world monopoly of English (just how English became the means of processing the sounds of jazz and rock is an amazing story which has not yet been written. I have hit upon it recently).

A "Centre for Understanding Media" need not include any new physical hardware. I have discovered that friends and acquaintances in many places are eager to use their existing operations, whether of broadcasting or business, to play host to a Centre. It would in effect be a great advantage to themselves to share media problems and insights around the world. This could be done on the side, as it were, without extra staff or office space. I have run my own Centre here in Toronto in that way, as an extra-curricular activity. What would be needed, in order to interlace a whole group of Centres, would be minimal means for publishing a periodic Digest of discoveries and problems relating to media and politics. My own preference would be to keep these things minimal and succinct and iconic. However, I assume that this is not the time or place to go into details.

Heartiest congratulations and good wishes for your unremitting excellence of performance.

Sincerely
Marshall

August 21, 1972.

Dear Marshall,

Thank you very much for your letter, which I have just had the chance to see after returning to Ottawa. Your idea of setting up "Centres for Understanding Media" is an interesting one but perhaps I might have some time to think about it.

As always, your kind remarks are very much appreciated.

Yours sincerely,
Pierre

1973

January 4, 1973

Dear Pierre:

May it be a blessed New Year for you and your family. We much enjoyed the greeting card with Justin's picture with "one shoe off and one shoe on."

During the 2015 Christmas season, the first as prime minister for Justin Trudeau, his mother talked to the press about this same greeting card: http://www.cbc.ca/news/politics/trudeau-baby-christmas-card-1.3371486.

I feel that I should not take up your time with ordinary verbiage. One of the effects of TV is to reduce the human attention span, which may explain why the one-line joke is in, and the old story-line joke is out. I am going to venture to send you, from time to time, some one-line jokes and observations that can serve your turn in a great variety of situations. Here, for example, are some one-liners apropos statistics:

Have you heard about the statistician who drowned while crossing a river whose <u>average</u> depth was six inches?

"If you put those figures on a rack, they will confess anything."

The <u>average</u> Canadian has one breast and one testicle.

Don't look back, they may be gaining on you!

Tarzan's last scream: "Who greased my vine?"

[M.M.]

January 5, 1973

Dear Pierre:

A one-liner that is very flexible in its uses goes: "As Zeus said to Narcissus: 'Watch yourself!'"

There is a basic political principle that may or may not be Hegelian in pattern. It follows the structure of the wheel and the axle. Between the wheel and the axle there must be "play". This play is "touch". When the interval between wheel and axle is too small, they seize up and there is neither wheel nor axle. When the interval is too large, the wheel falls off. The principle that the resonant interval between the wheel and the axle is where the action is would seem to apply quite well to war, and politics, and many social situations. Let me illustrate: the Western world is going Eastward via electricity. That is, it is going inward and abandoning its outer goals. The Eastern world, on the contrary, is going outward via our nineteenth-century technology and is acquiring outer goals and objectives. Between these two vast components moving antithetically, there is a resonant interval, a gap. As with the wheel and the axle, the gap is where the action is. At the moment, this gap is Viet Nam.

Is it not important to understand that Viet Nam is not a component nor an objective nor a target, but only a resonant interval or "interface"? In quantum mechanics the chemical bond is referred to as the resonant interval, since there are no connections. The same principle would seem to apply to the interface between political parties. That is, the action would take place in the gap between them. By the same token, Women's Lib would be the interval between masculine and feminine sexes or parties. The interval would be a gap of non-sex, "where the action is."

The ordinary instinct to speak of the business game, or the political game, would seem to be rooted in the awareness of "play" as crux in all forms of social action. It is a basic feature of play that it keeps us in touch, and is also extremely involving of our faculties. Paradoxically, there is also the principle of leisure involved in play, since it is only the specialist who works. When we are using only a small part of our faculties, we are working. When we are totally involved, we are playing. The artist is always at leisure, especially when most intensely engaged in making.

[M.M.]

January 17, 1973

Dear Pierre:

Corinne and I join in prayers and concern for you, especially at this time of the loss of your mother.[159]

Sincerely,
[M.M.]

Suzette
Pierre
Charles

deeply appreciate your kind
expression of sympathy
on the death of their mother
Mrs. Grace Elliott Trudeau

Montreal, January 1973

January 23, 1973.

Dear Marshall:

Thank you very much for your letters of January 4th and 5th. The one-liners are delightful and I certainly intend to keep them ready for the right occasion.

I was also very intrigued by your idea of the resonant interval being where the action is. It certainly describes well what is going on in the House of Commons at the moment.

It was kind of you to write and I will certainly be glad to get your future one-liners and observations.

With best wishes to you and your family,

Yours sincerely,
[M.M.]

159 Grace Elliott Trudeau (b. 1890) had died the day before.

February 12, 1973

Dear Pierre:

Just a word about interviews on the subject of your "arrogance".[160] Is it not relevant to ask the interviewer for help in clarifying the problem as it affects the supposed public that is represented by the interviewer? Are there not many hidden factors that the interviewer should explicate as part of his or her job in mediating between you and the public? For example, to the WASP world (white Anglo-Saxon Protestant) your mere existence as head of state is arrogant presumption. That is, for a French Catholic to rule over the "superior and dominant" group, represents to them a kind of reversal of nature, an upsetting of the relation between figure and ground, in gestalt terms.

Canada's head of state is royal, not elected – when this letter was written, that meant Queen Elizabeth II, as it still does. McLuhan was not making a mistake here, but a rhetorical point.

In a word, there is a wide spread assumption that your arrogance exists in merely occupying your present role. That is, it has nothing to do with your personal image but rather with your corporate role. As long as you were content to "put on" your public by playfulness and "clowning", it was felt that they did not have to take you seriously. As soon as you "play it straight", the WASP public feels abused, since it alone has the right to assume the mask of serious corporate power.

Note how Richard Nixon has ineptly tried to mitigate his crude and harsh image by liaison with various figures in the world of entertainment. He is quite unable to combine these qualities in himself in the way that you have done. To the WASP world the light-hearted approach to power represents aristocratic insouciance and security. The entertainer is a figure which they themselves have crowned. He is permitted to hurt them by his humour, for that is the mask of his power and relevance alike.

160 Another friend responded to the frequent charge of arrogance against Trudeau by writing, "His arrogance, if that is what it was, was saved for those whose questions and comments arose not from an interest in his answers but from a desire to score points." Cook, *Teeth of Time*, 46.

A great complication occurs in the matter of your image as it must be presented simultaneously to French and English. Our media totally ignore this fact. The obligations which you have to the French electorate seem to be much at odds with the forming of an image for effective relatedness to the WASP world. Neither on radio, TV, nor in the press is there ever the slightest hint that this problem exists. You are obliged to perform a balancing act on the high wire for two conflicting publics. It is very important that these publics should see each other at the same time that they are watching you, for their responses to you and to one another are totally diverse.

Cordially and
Prayerfully
Marshall

February 25, 1973

Dear Marshall:

I found your letter of February 12th very perceptive, as usual, but also applicable to my immediate actions. I plan to reflect on it, when next considering any public appearances. Perhaps even, I could even give a talk (in Ottawa) on the importance of the two publics you describe seeing "each other at the same time that they are watching (me)."

Many thanks for your thoughts and prayers. God bless.

Pierre

This letter was handwritten by Trudeau on personal stationery from the PM's official residence, 24 Sussex Drive, in Ottawa, and is the first to McLuhan in which he uses this kind of God-language. McLuhan used it right from his first letter to Trudeau, which concludes "with most cordial good wishes and prayers." This kind of relaxed natural God-talk between them increases with the years.

The religion of political leaders in Canada didn't carry the political importance given to it in other countries; it was a private matter, one that Trudeau, for example, rarely discussed in public. Of course, the assumption was that most politicians, and all prime ministers, were Christian, as all Canadian prime ministers have in fact been, but it never seemed relevant. Now I marvel at that naiveté, both collective and my own.

July 6, 1973

Dear Pierre:

A friend in Dallas phoned to suggest that I do a short piece on Mr. Nixon. It is somewhat tentative, but I enclose a copy in the event of its having some interest for you. Some of the most obvious features of the affair, like the civil war between the two secret services and the co-opting of national politics for summer network relief, I simply pass over.

Cordial good wishes for a recreative summer,
Marshall

July 10, 1973

Dear Pierre:

Last night's Toronto Star mentioned your having some doubts about the Canadian West and its strange attachment to the Mounties and the monarchy. As a Westerner, I can help to illuminate this matter. The West has always been on the defensive, if only because it is relatively uninhabited territory. Both the Mountie and the monarchy are figures, as it were, without a ground. They are lonely and isolated images, dedication without a cause.

There is a great vacuum between the Western provinces and the U.S. to the south, and this constitutes a sort of psychic frontier which is an area of intense interface and uncertainty and stress. This frontier lends itself to a great deal of creativity in vision and resourcefulness. As is only natural, it is a state which is least active in Vancouver, which is so close to the really populated U.S.A. that it can share some of the filled-in, comfortable outlook of Eastern Canadian cities that are close to the U.S.A. It would be quite easy to fill in this story with reference to Canadian writing and activities, but this would not be at all necessary for yourself.

Warm regards,
Marshall

August 14, 1973

Dear Pierre:

I hasten to enclose these thoughts on inflation and crowd dynamics[161] in the hope that they will be of direct aid to you in tackling the whole question.

Corinne and I rejoice in your current appearances as we follow them in the press.

Cordially
Marshall

August 24, 1973.

Dear Marshall:

You sent to me two most interesting pieces of information in early July – your article on Mr Nixon and the Drop Out Strategy and your illuminating explanation indeed with regard to my doubts about the Canadian West and its strange attachment to the Mounties and the Monarchy.

I wish I had been able to thank you sooner but the summer has been really hectic.

With appreciation and kindest personal regards,

Sincerely,
Pierre

161 "Media and the Inflation CROWD", which is apparently a play on "Inflation and the Crowd" by Elias Canetti, cited at the end of the piece.

August 27, 1973.

Dear Marshall,

Many thanks for your note of the 14th and for the accompanying copy of your paper.

Your perception of inflation as a psychological manifestation of crowd behavior in the market place is enlightening. When our government tried to combat the "inflation psychology" in 1969, I had to use strong words,[162] so that the crowd would be convinced that we would not back off in our fight. We succeeded better than most countries; but then my strong words were remembered, and the government became the direct culprit of other attendant economic evils.

Such a phenomenon not only makes it difficult to counter act inflation psychology; but perhaps explains why the crowd, led by the press, having through inflation experienced depreciation of self, then must ensure that the government and politicians are depreciated even more!

All the best to you both.

Cordially,
[P.E.T.]

October 17, 1973.

CONGRATULATIONS.
HAPPY BIRTHDAY AND
CONGRATULATIONS ON
CHINA TRIUMPH.

Marshall McLuhan

On October 10, Trudeau and a group that included Margaret, who was seven months pregnant, flew to the People's Republic of China, making him the first Canadian prime minister to visit the PRC. Alexandre Trudeau was born that Christmas.

162 For example: ""We can only get tougher, we can't get weaker… I'm afraid there are a lot of people who are bargaining that the Government can't act tough for too long because it will only get frightened if it sees unemployment go up to 6 percent. But if people think we are going to lose our nerve because of that, they should think again because we're not.' These unwise comments and his upturned finger to the striking Lapalme truck drivers in 1970 as he told them to 'eat shit' transformed Trudeau's image for many Canadians." English, *Just Watch Me*, 160.

October 31, 1973.

Dear Marshall:

I was pleased to receive your telegram wishing me a Happy Birthday and referring so enthusiastically to my trip to China. Do let me thank you for your thoughtfulness.

With kind regards,
Sincerely,
Pierre

1974

February 25, 1974

Dear Mr. McLuhan,

I apologize for this very late reply to a letter to Jim Davey, [a] copy of which came to me "for action" as they say in the Public Service.

I was very interested in your letter. I think you make a very good point. It was again brought home to me yesterday as I listened to an interview of the Prime Minister by André Payette on the French network, when the Prime Minister discussed the question of cultural sovereignty and the status of French in Quebec.

The shortest way to get a discussion going might be for you to get in touch with the people responsible for News and Public Affairs at the CBC and Radio-Canada.[163] At CBC, I would say that your man is Knowlton Nash.[164] At Radio-Canada, it's Marc Thibault. I, of course, will also keep in mind your views as it should be possible to take them into account when this Office discusses interviews with the networks.

I was also interested in your views on "the ordinary human pattern of going outside to be with people and inside to be alone". One of the Servan-Schreiber[165] brothers or cousins writes about this in a book called "Le Pouvoir d'Informer". Discussing newspapers and television, the author points to the fact that whereas in days past the citizen was

163 La Société Radio-Canada, the CBC's French-language arm, both radio and television.

164 Knowlton Nash (1927–2014), prominent broadcaster and journalist. In the course of my grade 12 media project, I spent part of a weekend at CBC-TV's newsmagazine show, *Weekend*, meeting not only Nash's right-hand man, John Kerr, but also coming across the name "Bob Frye," the show's senior producer. Decades later, Frye co-taught a Rutgers University Division of Global Affairs seminar in which I was enrolled.

165 Jean-Louis Servan-Schreiber (b.1937), French journalist and human rights activist, had a strong interest in Canada.

ready to run out of home to get the paper and thus be in touch with the world, he now runs back home to do the same.

We have been thinking here of using some of your one-liners for the Prime Minister's off-the-record Press Gallery meeting. I am sure we will find a way of giving you credit for them!

Sincerely,
Pierre O'Neil
Press Secretary

March 14, 1974

Dear Marshall:

I have heard that recently among your many honours, you have received a civic award of merit from the city of Toronto on the occasion of Toronto's 140th birthday.

Here's one occasion where it cannot be said 'A prophet has no honour in his own country.'[166]

Congratulations, Marshall, and as always, my best wishes.

Sincerely, and God bless!
Pierre

March 26, 1974

Dear Pierre:

There may be some relevance in the questions that Clare Boothe Luce[167] asked recently, and my replies. First, her questions:

1) How do you explain why Vatican II,[168] which closed in a burst of ecumenical fervor that was expected to revive the faith of the Catholic

---

166 A reference to the Gospel of John 4:44. Trudeau used the same thought, less cheerfully, in his April 28, 1980, letter to McLuhan.

167 Clare Boothe Luce, author and diplomat, converted to Catholicism in 1946.

168 More formally known as the Second Vatican Council, this influential meeting ran from 1962 to 1965. It addressed issues of Church renewal and relations with the non-Catholic world. It resonates still.

world in the Church's institutions and teachings was, instead, followed (and so soon) by the greatest loss of faith in them that we have seen since the Reformation? Was Vatican II the cause?

2) Please explain why you think (or don't think) that the impeachment of R.N. is going to purify democratic politics and "restore integrity" to Government, and how this will help us control inflation, pollution, repair the breach with NATO, etc.

3) What are your theories of money and of value? Why, for example, did those great Etruscan statues which stood for years in the Great Hall of the Met,[169] praised by all the critics and admired by all the populace, valued in nine figures, suddenly become valueless when they were discovered to be forgeries? Are Value and Money, like Beauty, in the eye of the beholder? Or, what other than life itself (and health in life) has intrinsic value?

****

Now, my replies to her questions:

Vatican II was a blossoming of liberal individualism and a kind of immolation of the individual in the great new involvement plunge made possible by the TV sensibility of inner-tripping. The moment that people become deeply involved they lose their private identity and their direction. If the Reformation was the tossing away of acoustic and musical hierarchies in favour of visual and private points of view, Vatican II was the burial of this kind of individualism in the newly created swamp of electronic togetherness and total involvement, as in a skin-flick where everybody gets inside one skin. In the novel Silence,[170] Shusaku Endo has an introduction explaining how impossible it is for Hellenistic or Western Christianity to find a foothold in the tribal or acoustic swamp of Japan. I have written in the Critic[171] and elsewhere, on this subject, asking Catholic philosophers and theologians to explain what successor to the Graeco-Roman literary tradition they foresee. The mystery

169 The Metropolitan Museum of Art in New York City.

170 A movie based on this 1969 book by Japanese Catholic writer Shusako Endo (1923–1996) and directed by Martin Scorsese was released in January 2017.

171 McLuhan's article "Do Americans Go to Church to Be Alone?" appeared in the January–February 1973 issue of *Critic*: 14–23.

of how the church was committed to this Graeco-Roman thing is quite beyond me, although I perceive it as providential, in the strict sense. Today, under electric conditions there's no way in which the Graeco-Roman tradition can survive in the West.

To use the terms of Ballandier who invented the phrase "the Third World", there is the First World of 19th century industrialism and the Second World of Russian Communism and the Third World is that which is left out of these benefits. But he forgot the Fourth World, the instantaneous global village which, since Sputnik (October, 1957),[172] created Spaceship Earth, an ecological entity, without passengers but only crew. The First World has as much trouble relating to the Fourth World of electronics as the Third World has in obtaining benefits from the First World of industrial hardware. On the other hand, the Third World has no trouble in relating to the acoustic and electronic Fourth World.

The magisterium of the church tends to become multi-locational and acoustic, with central Roman authority becoming difficult to imagine. Please note that I am doing now, as elsewhere, a structural or formal meditation on the situations we have encountered.

The Protestant strategy in the 16th century was to use the new portable book as a God-given means of escape from the Roman yoke. Rome used the book in the opposite way, as a means of standardizing and centralizing by uniformity. The law of implementation is always to use the new thing for the old purpose, while ignoring that the new thing tends to destroy the old purposes. I have discovered over the years that the effects of innovation are always subliminal, and people resent having this pointed out, feeling that you are invading their privacy in so doing.

Let us turn, then, to your question about the impeachment of Richard Nixon. Nixon and the U.S.A. are caught between the First World and the Fourth World. That is, while having all its commitments to the old Graeco-Roman hardware, it is totally involved in the new electronic information environment which is dissolving all the controls and all the goals of the First World. The Fourth World, or the electronic

172 Sputnik 1, the first artificial satellite, was launched by the U.S.S.R. on October 14, 1957. The event also launched the space age and the space race between the U.S.A. and the Soviet Union.

world, reduces personal identity profiles to vestigial level and, by the same token, reduces moral commitments in the private sector almost to zero. Paradoxically, however, as private morals in the private sector sink down, new absolutist demands are made of ethics in the public or political sector. R.N. had the misfortune to bring the old private morals into the public place just when this reversal had occurred. There is also the misfortune of his image which is intensely private and non-corporate and therefore totally unsuited to TV. (Charisma is looking like a lot of the people – anything except one's self!)

The U.S., the only great country in the world based on a written constitution, has no way of coping legally or politically with the new oral and acoustic situations created by the electronic bugging and the general X-ray procedures in the entire private sector. Man-hunting has become the biggest business on the planet in the electronic age, and is a return to the Paleolithic conditions of the hunter. The impeachment threat represents the rage of the literate media against the new electric environment which has invaded their world and corrupted all their values. I would like very much to explain in more detail the clash between written and oral patterns to commitment in society and politics and personal life alike.

You ask also about inflation and pollution and the breach with NATO, etc. I have an unpublished paper in which I try to explain that inflation also is the encounter of incompatible worlds, the clash between the old commodity markets and the new money, or information markets. Money as information, and investment, now moves at instant speeds, putting an unbearable strain and rim-spin, as it were, on the old price system with its quantified commodities. This huge disproportion between the old speeds of the hardware world and the instant electric speeds of the software Fourth World extends to our private lives as much as to our social existence. It is impossible to retain private goals in an instant world. One must flip instead into role-playing, which means submergence in corporate situations. Strange that I should be mentioning these things today when I am going to introduce Eric Havelock to a University of Toronto audience. In his Preface to Plato (Oxford University Press, 1963) he explains how the phonetic alphabet evoked a private image of the substantial individual. I understand this much better now than even he explains it. The unique technology of the phonetic alphabet was the fact that its components were phonemes (meaningless bits) rather than morphemes (meaningful bits). Magically, the fission of the phonetic alphabet is to isolate the visual sensory factor from all other senses, and to constitute the image of the private person. We are now playing this drama in reverse in the electric age.

Your questions about my theories of money and value and the Etruscan forgeries would take a little while to elaborate. Let me mention, however, that we live in the age of the "genuine fake" because we understand for the first time the art process and the making process as never before, so that Picasso said long ago: "I always paint fakes". The function of art in relating us to ourselves and to our world and in freeing us from the adaptive or robot role, has changed entirely in the electric time. The art product as such becomes relatively insignificant compared to the process of making and of participation in that making. What you mention as the "value" of the Etruscan images, relates very much to their commodity character in the First World of industrial hardware. In that world they stood for the antithesis and, therefore, the ideal of industrialism. Hypocritically, the First World worshipped art as its own opposite. The Etruscans themselves would have agreed with the Balinese who say: "We have no art. We do everything as well as possible." Or, they would agree with a local junkyard sign which read: "Help beautify junkyards. Throw something lovely away today."

You are most generous in even noticing my Civic Award, and it is quite princely of you to have written me about it. Mrs. McLuhan joins me in heartiest and most cordial regards to you and your family.

P.S. In the cause of bilingualism, I enclose a new book made by a friend of mine who is a former Professor of French here at the University of Toronto.[173] It seems to me to hold the promise of a live TV show in which French idioms are presented both acoustically and visually.

[M.M.]

173 Alta Lind Cook, whose book, *Daisy*, was published in 1974. There is a notation near the top of the letter, in pencil, that the letter had arrived with a copy of a book of that name.

March 29, 1974.

Dear Marshall,

I thoroughly enjoyed reading your letter of the 26th.

Your 'First, Second, Third and Fourth Worlds' framework for the purpose of analyzing current events and determining public attitudes is intriguing and fascinating. What you said about money and value theories and your reference to "genuine fakes" reminded me of Clifford Irving's contribution to the age you speak of. His biography of Howard Hughes – himself often thought no longer to be alive – is now known to be a fake, and his first best-seller, Fake, was about the life of Elmyr de Hory who gave untold happiness to hundreds by selling them fake Impressionists which he didn't copy but created!

Thank you very much for sending me a copy of Alta Lind Cook's Daisy; it is utterly delightful. Please congratulate Miss Cook for me when you next speak to her.

All the best to you and to Mrs. McLuhan.

Pierre

April 3, 1974

Dear Pierre:

I see by the papers that there is, and will continue to be, a great deal of confusion about streaking. It is just possible that I can be of some help here. The streaker[174] is a "put on" in the same way that the stripper is. She takes off her clothes in order to "put on" her audience. Though nude, she is completely clad in her audience, as much as a model in a life class. It is when she steps backstage that she is naked, or minus her audience.

174 The Oxford version notes that "streaker" means "nude runner." Molinaro, Corinne McLuhan and Toye, eds., *Letters*, 496.

The streaker is putting on his audience because he wishes to be seen. He is a role-player and not a private person, therefore he hides his face and his name. His "put on" has to do with a grievance against what he feels to be a hypocritical society. The streaker and the striker are near kin, only the striker strips off the services which are the social clothing in order to "put on" his audience. It would be easy to enlarge this theme, but probably not necessary. The moral issue of decency or indecency is really irrelevant in view of streaking as essentially a political act of defiance and rebellion.

[M.M.]

April 8, 1974.

Dear Marshall:

Many thanks for yours of the 3rd. The explanation you offer as to the why of streaking makes a lot of sense.

One thing though: why do you say that streaking is an essentially <u>political</u> act of defiance? To me, there is an even greater element of rebellion against social values in this latest fad.

All the best.

Sincerely,
Pierre

June 13, 1974

Dear Pierre:

Just a note to indicate one very effective way of dealing with hecklers. Beckon him to come forward to the microphone and not to waste his sweetness on the desert air, as it were. There might be an occasional heckler who had a speech ready for such an occasion, but it shuts up 99% of them instantly. It is a way of turning the tables, and compels the heckler to "put on" the public instead of "putting on" the speaker. There's a great gap between using the speaker as a captive audience and using the captive audience as a public.

The government had recently instigated its own downfall (Trudeau, *Memoirs*, 176) and an election had been called for July 8 (the Liberals won a majority). The letter is often quoted because of McLuhan's advice about hecklers, but to me it is more important in exposing the prime minister, possibly for the first time, to McLuhan's astute ideas about work, gender roles and specialization in the electronic age. Some of McLuhan's comments elsewhere about women can be less agreeable.

Apropos your query about streaking as social rather than political defiance, I agree, since I was using the word "political" to cover social forms as well.

Recently, I was in Stockholm to give some talks and I discovered that Scandinavia is the world in which North American hippies would be at home. The reason for this lies in the fact that Scandinavians have very low identity profiles. They are real "cool" in the sense of being group-oriented rather than private goal-seekers. They originated the ombudsman,[175] and think of themselves as dedicated to helping the little people like themselves. Wouldn't you say that our own rebellious youngsters are "nobodies" who resent having to share the establishment with the somebodies of yesterday? That is, the young people with very low identity profiles[176] find it difficult to accept jobs or roles in which high identity is expected. Is it not Nixon's earnestness and specialist goal-seeking that alienates him from the new generation?

May I venture to suggest also an approach to the women's lib matter? Women are less specialized than men, and long accustomed to adapting to a variety of roles. In our new instant-information environment, most men who have been accustomed to specialist jobs and functions must now switch from role to role in the course of a day. In the big hierarchies this creates extreme discomfort and dismay, and it is increasingly obvious that women could perform many of these functions better than

175 Most of "ombudsman" has been underlined by a reader.

176 There is a notation here by someone (i.e. TV generation).

men. However, when a woman is compelled to assume the job[177] of a customs or immigration official, she becomes the specialist monster, the very antithesis of role-playing. Yet we consider it natural for men to perform these specialist functions.

Prayerfully
Marshall

September 20, 1974

Dear Pierre:

Friends in the Ontario government told me yesterday that Davis[178] is moving for an immediate snap election to prevent any opposition organization and to anticipate the unpopularity he foresees resulting from economic impasse. I enclose a small essay on inflation in which I propose the only dis-equilibrium theory, so far as I know.

Corinne and I are naturally distressed at Margaret's illness, and we shall pray.

yrs Marshall

Three days earlier, the news had featured Margaret's release from Royal Victoria Hospital in Montreal and the first public inklings that she might have mental health problems. In the years since, Margaret Trudeau has become a mental health advocate and has written of her own struggles with bipolar disorder.

177 This has been changed, by hand, from "role."

178 William Davis, Conservative premier of Ontario from 1971 to 1985.

September 26, 1974.

Dear Marshall,

A short note but I do want to thank you for your thoughtful letter of September 20 and for your essay on inflation – it is on my list of priority reading and study material.

I also owe you my thanks for your letter of June 13. I was absent from Ottawa almost continuously during the last two weeks of June and did not read your letter until after the election. It is a strange coincidence, but I fairly well followed your recommendation about the handling of hecklers, at a public meeting in Peterborough on July 6.

With my deep gratitude to you and Corinne for the prayers you are saying for Margaret – the latest news is encouraging.

Sincerely, and God bless!
Pierre

1975

January 22, 1975

Dear Pierre:

Apropos my inflation piece, which you mentioned you might show to John Turner,[179] two articles on multi-national corporations in the New Yorker for December 2nd and 9th drew attention to some of the ways that they avoid the equilibrium operations of our own commodity markets by direct "transfer trading" among themselves. Computerized book-keeping enables them to "cook the books" in such a way as to accommodate them to a wide range of needs. A separate set with [a] unique "bottom line" is kept for each government and each government department so that there is no question of their ever paying any income tax.

It is computerized book-keeping that by-passes the structure of the old industrial markets of nineteenth century hardware, rendering Keynesian strategies helpless. That is, the computer is an electric form that is able to transcend the structure of the "First World" arrangements. (i.e., the "First World" = the Western industrial set-up, the "Second World" = Russian socialism, the "Third World" = all those countries without a nineteenth century, and the "Fourth World" = the electric information world which goes around all of them, having quite different effects on each.)

We shall persist in our prayers for you and Margaret.

[M.M.]

179 Finance minister John Turner succeeded Trudeau in 1984 as Liberal Party leader and prime minister, but served only 80 days before being defeated in an election.

February 14, 1975

Dear Pierre:

Wishing not to take up your time and attention beyond a minimum, let me point to one of the big shifts now current in life and society. The split between work and residence which came with industrial specialism and division of labour is ending swiftly with the new electric environment of software information. The return to human scale and human involvement is getting spectacular play in the Thatcher[180] episode, but it has also invaded the entire range of young people's attitudes and interests. Women's Lib belongs very much in the shift from specialist job-holding to multiple role-playing.

Another major pattern appears with the multi-national corporations who use the new computer technology to play the old game of equilibrium economics. By leaping across national and market boundaries, they by-pass the old controls that had been developed in those separate areas. "Transfer pricing" is the name they use for this by-pass. No new controls have been invented to restrain their arbitrary price-setting. These arbitrary tactics have long been the practice in the Second World of socialist Russia. Equilibrium, which works within a single market or single nation, is completely disrupted when these boundaries are transcended. We are, therefore, in the position of watching the new electric information speed dissolve the structures of the old hardware, which moves very slowly. Systems analysis, in the same way, applies electric speed to older organization patterns, eliminating human scale and relationships.

Ever in our prayers
yrs Marshall

---

180 Margaret Thatcher, prime minister of Great Britain from 1979 to 1990, had been elected leader of the Conservative Party three days earlier.

February 17, 1975.

Dear Marshall

Many thanks for your letter of January 22 commenting about the two articles on multi-national corporations which appeared in the December 2 and 9, 1974 issues of the New Yorker.

Your remarks are typically incisive. I have been able to secure a copy of the articles and propose to give them a careful reading.

Margaret and I are grateful to you and Corinne for your continued prayers. With warm regards to you both.

Sincerely,
Pierre

March 17, 1975.

Dear Marshall,

Your most recent "signal and warning" reached my desk on the eve of my departure for an almost three-week official trip to Europe.

If I understand you well, the "global village" is characterized by a significant tension between "the return to human scale and human involvement", on the one hand, and the use of technology to "eliminate human scale and relationships", on the other. For my part, I feel confident that political man as such (and in my view every adult citizen should be a political man in the best sense of the term) is not inevitably doomed to the passive observer status! Your remarks remind me of the French philosopher Paul Ricoeur's comments on the bearing which apparently neutral, innocuous economic planning does have on our innermost personal values as well as on our way of life. When I think back on my college years, I wonder how Lucretius' aloofness could ever lull anyone from keeping on the alert! Do you recall:

"Suave, mari magno turbantibus aequora ventis,
E terra magnum alterius spectare laborem;
Non quia vexari quenquamst iucunda voluptas,
Sed quibus ipse malis careas quia cernere
suave est."?
De Rerum Natura,
ii, I.

(Sweet it is, when on the great sea the winds
are buffeting the waters,
To gaze from the land on another's great
struggles;
Not because it is pleasure or joy that any
one should be distressed;
But because it is sweet to perceive from
what misfortune you yourself are free."

(Trans. by Bailey).

Well, being above all an adamant optimist, I am strongly convinced that this tension can be turned into a most creative force, so that the "global village" will gradually take shape as a true city, i.e. a place worth living for all mankind. Please go on helping us to keep on the alert!

You too are ever in my prayers and in Margaret's as well.

Yours,
Pierre

July 2, 1975

Dear Pierre:

I think this may be a rather important note, and its brevity should be no indication of its significance. Apropos the problem of hanging and capital punishment, there seems to be a universal assumption that hanging is punitive, retaliation for misdeeds. I suggest that this is a very minor aspect of the matter. The central significance of capital punishment is the ritual that it entails, and this ritual serves primarily to enhance the significance and importance of human life by drawing attention to the decisive and infinite implications of the moment of death. If this is taken to concern capital punishment as figure, let us consider the ground that supports that figure or procedure.

We live in a time when the coalescing of all people on earth into a single mass-public has diminished human private identity almost to the vanishing point. Anybody at a ball game, for example, is a nobody, and the entire planet has become our ball park. Under electric conditions of our inter-involvement of all mankind, the information environment has blanketed and smothered private identity. This effect has made human life appear very cheap indeed. The TV generation cannot feel very much importance attaching to the private person. On the other hand, the loss of private identity which has come rather suddenly upon Western man has produced a deep anger at this rip-off of his private self.

There are two kinds of violence relating to the same situation, first, the kind that comes from the unimportance of everybody, and second, the kind that comes from the impulse to restore one's private meaning by acts of violence. On the frontier everybody is a nobody and violence is the order of the day. Electronic man lives on such a frontier at all times, doubting his identity and his survival alike. Psychologically considered, violence is an attempt to restore order to achieve identity.

With prayers for you and Margaret
Yrs Marshall

July 21, 1975

Dear Marshall,

As your letters to me always are, your latest note is thought-provoking. But I find it hard to follow your thinking all the way through it. You seem to take the paradox to the point of contradiction! (Unless I am less perceptive at the end of the House session… or because of the extreme "density" of your note.) For instance, your last paragraph: if it were true that "On the frontier everybody is a nobody", I would assume that "indifference" in respect of life and death (and consequently, comfortable suicide – like Petrone's[181] – and euthanasia) would be the order of the day, not violence which, in your logic, is a tribute to the value of life ("I don't want to be a nobody. But the only way of being somebody is to commit murder"...) I would rather subscribe to the following explanation: material comfort, social conformity, monotonous and repetitive jobs generate frustrations and aggressions for which our culture (or social organization) does not provide enough creative outlets, and destructive behaviours are the result. Konrad Lorenz's thesis seems illuminating in this regard: even when all basic needs are satisfied and the fight for freedom from (starvation, natural fears, plague, etc.) is no longer necessary, there is still a need to fight and to relieve aggressions. The problem: in a creative way. And in the wake of Paul Ricoeur and Erich Fromm, I would stress that daily work and general working conditions should, as such, be creative outlets. In other words, creative opportunities must exist in more than just special hobbies or occasional ventures... Otherwise, as Ricoeur points out, we mostly "live in deferment".

Well, I find myself lecturing you. That should suffice for the time being!

Margaret joins me in wishing you and Corinne all the very best.

Sincerely,
Pierre

July 30, 1975

Dear Pierre:

When you reply to my letters, I feel extremely selfish for taking any of your time at all. However, I feel obliged to clarify the theme of violence and capital punishment, if possible. Rollo May has a book – Power and Innocence – in which the theme is my own, namely, that violence in its innumerable modalities is typically a response to loss of identity or to a

181 Gaius Petronius Arbiter (c. 27–66 BCE), author of the comic novel *Satyricon*.

threat against one's self, or one's thought. Technical innovations, simply by creating new environments, upset people's images of themselves. The bigger the technology, the bigger the upset, and the bigger the threat to one's image. The image can be private or corporate.

All this relates to the other situation I mentioned, namely, that one's image of one's self at a ball game is minimal. The most important figure in the world is a nobody at a ball game. Electronically, however, all of us are attending the same ball game in the same ball park, namely, Spaceship Earth. Our involvement in each other has become so intense that our private image has been reduced to the minimum. The universal response is one of anger and violence, which is not made the less by the mysteries and unexpected rip-off of the private self which has taken place. Violence is a natural attempt to re-establish and to re-discover the nature of one's being. The Scripture tells us that "the King of Heaven doth suffereth violence, for there the least shall be the most."[182]

My other thought in this matter concerned capital punishment as a <u>means</u> of re-establishing the importance and dignity of individuals. I am not advocating capital punishment, but I am pointing to its effects in enhancing the significance of the human drama of life and death. At present, the legal procedures of trial and incarceration for murder seem to multiply the sheer quantity of bureaucratic activity while withdrawing all dignity from the participants. When you say: "I would rather subscribe to the following explanation: material comfort, social conformity, monotonous and repetitive jobs generate frustrations and aggressions for which our culture (or social organization) does not provide enough creative outlets, and destructive behaviours are the result", I certainly agree with you. However, this situation is itself a monstrous rip-off of private identity. I also agree with your idea of the problem as one which demands creative outlets. However, I seem to be saying that the ritual of capital punishment, carried out in the most public possible way, is itself an intensively creative outlet for the entire society.

Our daughter Teri, whom you met, has spent the last three weeks at the Moscow Film Festival. Her picture on Curtis, the photographer of North American Indians, having been one of three North American

182 This seems to be a conflation of verses from the Gospel of Matthew.

films chosen by the Russians, for their Festival. She has certainly found her creative outlet, though it has entailed some very vicious competition and frustration.

One of the strange things I have discovered about my own work is that Westerners in general resent having the effects of any technology brought to their attention. That print, or the telephone, or TV should have any effect on them at all, is taken to mean that they have been manipulated and degraded. The person who is blamed for this, is the person who points it out to them.

I enclose two or three jests which I hope you will find usable.

[M.M.]

October 14, 1975.

Dear Marshall,

You shouldn't feel selfish for "taking any of my time at all" in writing to me. I do enjoy reading and answering your letters.

The Trudeaus' third child, Michel, had been born 12 days earlier.

Since receiving your July 30th one, I have been able to follow up your reference to Rollo May's book on Power and Innocence. Chapters 6-9 helped me get a better grasp of what you were trying to put across in your previous of July 2nd about violence and capital punishment. So too did the further elaboration you offered on the comments you made in this previous one.

I am – at least intellectually – prepared to accept as a crude fact of our present civilization that "the ritual of capital punishment, carried out in the most public possible way, is itself an intensely creative outlet for the entire society", as you write. But I cannot help deplore such a "fact" (or "necessity") as a serious symptom of "collective insanity", to which remedies other than capital punishment can and will, I hope, be determined and applied in the not too distant future. And in so "deploring", I am in no way resentful about such a fact being made known to me, nor am I inclined to place any blame on the sharp-minded thinkers and socio-analysts who apprise me of it! (By the way, "this strange" reaction of resentment and blame to bad news or to the "prophet of evil" seems to resist all technological changes, even the most sophisticated ones: in this regard, I have just read a few relevant remarks in French demographer Alfred Sauvy's most recent book, La fin des riches (p. 253 ss.). In the footsteps of scores of others, Sauvy substantiates in his own way the views of Gaston Bachelard in his La formation de l'esprit scientifique, contribution à une psychanalyse de la connaissance objective.

In closing, I must say how pleased I was to learn about the creative outlet… and frustration (!) your Teri found at the Moscow Film Festival. Please pass along my warmest congratulations for her so successful picture on Curtis. Your "jests" were, indeed, highly refreshing: I will look forward to making use of them on an "appropriate occasion".

Margaret joins me in wishing you all the very best.

I cannot end this letter without a reference to our friend Jim Davey, since he and I so enjoyed discussing your letters together. He left us at a time when we in the government needed his counsel badly. But then, there is no time when a man like Jim isn't needed… I am sure he is helping us, and Pat and the family, with his prayers.

In friendship
Pierre[183]

183 The salutation, and everything from the beginning of the final paragraph through the signature, are handwritten. Davey had died that summer after falling from the roof of his home while removing storm windows. Cook, *Teeth of Time*, 162.

1976

September 3, 1976

Dear Pierre:

The enclosures[184] may help you to follow my work more easily. For thirty years at least, I have been using the two hemisphere approach under the names of the written and the oral, the visual and the acoustic, the hot and the cool, the medium and the message, figure and ground, and so on. Now it turns out that medicine has been building a great beach-head for this approach with its new understanding of the two hemispheres of the brain. If you look at the traits of the left hemisphere, you will discover the lineaments of the First world – the literate and industrial world – and, on the other hand, in the right hemisphere you will perceive the characteristics of the Third world – the world without the phonetic alphabet.

The correspondence resumes after almost a year. McLuhan was on sabbatical, though busy with many projects. His health continued to decline and he suffered at least one small stroke, the morning after filming his part in the movie *Annie Hall*, a bit part, playing himself, that fixed "an image of him in viewers' minds to a surprisingly lasting degree." (Marchand, *Marshall McLuhan*, 271). Trudeau was dealing not only with what might be called the normal political routine, but also with the summer Olympic Games in Montreal (which included a Royal Visit), Canada's new status as a G7 nation, the ongoing disintegration of his marriage and the surging separatist Parti Québécois in Quebec.

During the past century, while the knowledge of the two hemispheres has been growing, there has also been a new electronic milieu

184 One enclosure was a photocopy of "The Other Hemisphere" by Robert J. Trotter from *Science News* (vol. 109), April 3, 1976, 218–223. The other was an apparently unpublished January 1967 piece by J.J. Dronkers, "The Great Train Robbery."

or environment which automatically pushes the right hemisphere into a more dominant position than it has held in the Western world since the invention of the phonetic alphabet. The two hemispheres naturally respond to the milieu or total surround in which people live and work. My work has been a dialogue between the two hemispheres in which the characteristics of the right hemisphere are given so much recognition that I have been unintelligible to the left hemisphere people. It happens that the left hemisphere people are completely out of touch with the results and the formal characteristics of their own new electric technologies.

Courage!
yrs Marshall

October 4, 1976.

Dear Marshall,

Thank you very much for your letter of September 3. I appreciate your thoughtfulness in keeping me informed about your work.

As always, I find your pioneering in ideas to be most stimulating, although, I must admit, not always effortlessly grasped. Your perspective challenges us to reach towards a fuller understanding of ourselves and the world we've created.

With best wishes, and God bless,
Pierre

November 26, 1976

Dear Pierre:

I have been "under the weather", but keeping my eye on the all-too-interesting developments in our Canadian world. This includes prayers for you and Margaret.

I enclose a few pages sent to me by Tony Schwartz, an old friend and follower of mine who is now a recognized maestro in managing media in political terms. He has a little book called The Responsive Chord (New York: Anchor Press, 1973) which relates to many of these matters, and his page 14 states that "TV uses the eye as an ear." He is one of the very few who really understands that TV is not merely a visual medium. His late intervention may well have turned the trick for Carter.

Heartiest good wishes,
(dictated by telephone and signed in Professor McLuhan's absence)

On November 2, Jimmy Carter, McLuhan's "second-favorite politician," had been elected president of the United States. On November 15, the Parti Québécois, under the leadership of René Lévesque, with whom Trudeau had a long and complicated relationship, won the provincial election in Quebec.

Sound pioneer and media theorist Tony Schwartz was a creator of the "daisy ad," widely credited with helping Lyndon Johnson defeat Barry Goldwater for the U.S. presidency in 1964.

http://www.nytimes.com/2008/06/17/business/media/16cnd-schwartz.html?pagewanted=all&_r=0

During an October 2017 program at Fordham University, marking 50 years since McLuhan taught there, Professor John Carey said the chief technology officer in the Obama presidential campaigns told him *The Responsive Chord* had been required reading for the communication team.

December 13, 1976.

Dear Marshall.

I am sorry to hear that you have not been well and hope that you are steadily improving. I appreciate your taking the time to send me the interesting articles on the use of television in the American presidential campaign. As ever, I rely on you to keep me informed of developments in the field of communications.

With best personal regards, and prayers,

Yours sincerely,
[P.E.T.]

1977

February 14, 1977

Dear Pierre:

This is a note on the structural reasons for the P.Q. success.[185] Barrington Nevitt (the management consultant with whom I did The Executive as Dropout) and I are doing an essay on the P.Q. thing, which we will send to you shortly.

What has been missed by all parties to the discussion is the hidden ground that underlies not only the Canadian but the world structure in politics. Without exception, all the 19th century patterns of relatedness or of centralism are being reversed by the sheer speed-up of information. In terms of the twin hemispheres of the brain, the new ground of instant information pushes the right hemisphere of the brain up into dominance. In the Third World this is not especially noticeable since they have a dominant right hemisphere at all times. However, it is very noticeable in the First World since it upsets all existing organizations of family, education, business and politics alike. The left hemisphere which has been dominant in the First World for centuries, is lineal and logical and quantitative and goal-oriented. The right hemisphere is simultaneous, oral, acoustic, intuitive and qualitative. The upsurge of this long neglected hemisphere brought Jimmy Carter to the White House with a black vote. Jimmy is the first President from the deep South, the oral territory of the U.S.A., the place where jazz and rock and roll originate.

The hidden ground of instant information, which is as prevalent as transistor radios, automatically collapses the organization chart in all its forms, whether in classroom curriculum or in family life and bureaucracy alike. Dropout-ism, in all its forms, is the result of speed-

185 On November 15, the separatist Parti Québécois had won its first provincial election in Quebec.

up of information and the resulting reversal of patterns, e.g., Women's Lib, and also the powerful return of the oral tradition in Quebec. The same forces that make Roots the top show on TV, make French nostalgia for independence and tradition a major fact. The sociologists with whom you have talked, pay no attention to hidden ground or the new subliminal factor in this electronic time. Scientists and sociologists are trained to look only at the figure, not the ground. They quantify, and count noses, and ignore patterns of change. The instant or simultaneous is necessarily oral and acoustic, so that all forms of lineal and connected and logical discourse yield to the analogical and the imaginative. Separatism is at present a planetary phenomenon, familiar inside every home and every community and every nation.

Prayers and good wishes,

[M.M.]

P.S. I should add that at every level and in every situation the dropout, whether individual or group, is in search of an identity. Violence accompanies the quest for identity. On the frontier (Westerns) everybody is a nobody, ergo, everybody is rough and tough and in search of an identity.

February 24, 1977

Dear Pierre:

Everybody I know has been deeply thrilled by your recent performance and reception in the U.S. That was a really imaginative and masterly approach, which you brought off superbly.

It was while I was trying to explain charisma, as manifested by Jack Kennedy[186] and also by Jimmy

The "performance" was Trudeau's state visit to Washington, undertaken "primarily to counter a reassuring speech René Lévesque had made the previous month to the Economic Club in New York about Quebec independence." Guests at the state dinner included "Bill Clinton and Hillary Rodham." (English, *Just Watch Me*, 324.)

186 John Fitzgerald "Jack" Kennedy, president of the United States from 1961 until his assassination on November 22, 1963.

Carter, that I raised the fact of your very powerful charisma. Jack Kennedy looked like the all-American boy, the corporate, inclusive image of American ideals. Nixon, on the other hand, looked like himself alone, a private image, fatally defective in the TV age. In contrast, Jimmy Carter has the charisma of a Huck Finn,[187] a Southern boy, and he also has the vocal rhythms and corporate power that got him the black vote. It was while I was explaining these things that the interviewer asked: "What about Pierre Trudeau?" I replied that your corporate mask, your charisma, is both powerful and very popular with the young, in part because of the subtle hint in your image or "mask" of the native Indian. As you know, the Red man is very powerful with the TV generation since he is Third World, and they are also Third World. He was always Third World, but they, the young, are having their first experience of it. Naturally, pulled out of the context of this image discussion, it sounds very different, and even derogatory. You know me well enough to know that I would never say anything derogatory about you.

In the case of Carter, it became clear during the election that the image has supplanted the policy. A political point of view is not practical on TV since it is a resonating, multi-positional image, so that any moment of arrest or stasis permits the public to shoot you down. Maybe that is the meaning of the old gangster quote: "Talk fast, Mister!", and also, "Smile when you say that!" I have yet to find a situation in which there is not great help in the phrase: "You think my fallacy is all wrong?" It is literally disarming, pulling the ground out from under every situation! It can be said with a certain amount of poignancy and mock deliberation.

I am doing a piece about separatism and media in collaboration with Barrington Nevitt. He's the management consultant with whom I did the book on The Executive as Dropout. Our piece draws attention to the hidden ground that underlies all the many forms of separatism in our time. I refer to the ground of instant information that extends to the entire planet, and the effect of which is not centralism but decentralism. Any form pushed to its limit, as is pointed out by Aristotle and Aquinas, flips into the opposite form. Whereas hardware communication is a kind

187 The classic 19th-century American novel *Adventures of Huckleberry Finn*, by Mark Twain.

of transportation which centralizes organizational structures, electric communication is simultaneous and confers autonomy on every part of a structure. That is why the executive drops out of the old organization-chart patterns at electric speed. At electric speed, which is the speed of light, we are disembodied beings. On the phone, or "on the air", we are instantly present, but minus our bodies. Politically, discarnate man may have an image, but not a physical body. There is a corresponding loss of personal identity and responsibility which creates separatism in private life and family life and in all institutional existence. When one becomes aware of this hidden ground and its effects, one should be better prepared to cope with, and to counteract, these effects. Ours is surely the first human generation that has ever encountered such an undermining disease which afflicts us at all levels of church and state.

[M.M.]

April 4, 1977

Dear Pierre,

I enclose my meditations on the relations of French Canada and English Canada. Perhaps the two new things I have to say, concern the hidden effects of the ground of simultaneous information around the world, on the one hand, and the parallel to the secession of Quebec and the secession of the American South a century ago, on the other hand. In both cases the predominance of the oral culture vis-à-vis a written culture, was the decisive factor. Oral culture has been enormously enhanced by the electronic environment.

It is obvious that prayer is going to have more to do with easing this matter than human wisdom. I know, however, that you, for one, will bring a great deal of wisdom to bear.

Yrs Marshall

May 11, 1977

Dear Pierre:

Recently, at a Pro-Life Conference in Ottawa, it dawned on me that the peculiar character of discarnate man stems from his non-relation to "Natural" law. The mere fact of being disembodied, as we are in dreams, dissolves the relation to Nature and to "Natural" law. In the TV age especially, it is notable that the young feel few ties to external and private morality. I enclose a note on this subject.

[M.M.]

May 14, 1977

Dear Pierre,

I have been especially interested in the multi-culturalism of late since my daughter Teri is working on a feature film on this same theme. She is shooting the film on Cape Breton because of its tradition of French-Scottish dualism. Teri is a twin, and this picture concerns twin people and twin cultures.

Currently she is working on the film with Patrick Watson in Ottawa, and she plans to call you within the next few days. You may recall that she had dinner with us about four years ago at the Provençal here in Toronto.[188]

Teri's documentary film on North American Indians, The Shadow Catcher has received much international attention. Her new film will make a big contribution toward understanding the Canadian situation – the cultural one.

(My secretary is off duty on weekends!)

Yours,
Marshall

---

188 This paragraph has been marked out with a handwritten vertical line along the left side.

July 25, 1977

Dear Marshall,

Thank you for your May 11 letter and the enclosed note. I apologize for the delay in replying.

On March 4, the Trudeaus had begun a trial separation, instigated by Margaret, which was not made public. On May 30, the Prime Minister's Office officially announced their permanent separation. (English, *Just Watch Me*, 325.)

Everything in this letter from "and in friendship" was handwritten.

You continue to fascinate us with your treatises on the interaction and interrelation between technology and man. Your recent thoughts on the effects of the media on private morality present provocative though frightening observations of our society. One begins to wonder if our age of rapid communication leaves room for anything private – not just morality but thoughts and even creativity.

I welcome your correspondence, Marshall. You open to me an opportunity to turn my thoughts to different channels. I look forward to hearing more on your ideas of "private" morality.

Yours sincerely, and in friendship,
Pierre

When I was twenty, I was greatly influenced by Christian humanists like Maritain, and Christian existentialists like Mounier and Berdiaeff, who – in reaction to Descartes'[189] *dualism – were teaching us to "incarnate" our souls into our bodies, and hence to better relate to Natural Law.*

The T.V. age has created a new dualism, but the disembodiment is just as effective as the cartesian one. Can we get the T.V. generation interested in books? In natural law? In private morality?

P.

189 French philosopher René Descartes (1596–1650) can be considered the father of modern Western philosophy.

August 5, 1977

Dear Pierre,

I enclose [a] copy of a letter that you may find interesting.[190] Arthur Hurst[191] and I have been working for fifteen years on this problem, and only recently have we realized that Dyslexia and the loss of motor skills is directly related to television. Television is a disembodied experience. Being "on the air" is like being "on the phone" – one has no physical body.

Sincerely,
Marshall McLuhan

December 13, 1977

Dear Pierre:

We deeply appreciated your princely hospitality at the "Three Little Rooms",[192] and your presence at our seminar left a very deep impression of your cordial and lively person.

One of the things we have been working over in the seminar has been the problem of inflation and joblessness, two closely related things. To put both matters very briefly, the nature of work has changed drastically since we have begun to live in a simultaneous information environment. By the same token, the nature and function of money has been greatly altered by the electric information environment. Apropos work, the repetitive nine-to-five job has shifted into a new pattern of role-playing, which means a variety of functions, e.g. a mother doesn't have a job, she has fifty jobs, i.e., a role. The major form of work in the electronic age has become "keeping an eye on other people", whether

190 The letter is addressed to Edmund Gerald "Jerry" Brown, Jr., governor of California.

191 William Arthur Hurst, an optometrist in Newmarket, Ontario, also became a research associate at McLuhan's Centre.

192 Three Small Rooms, a popular upscale restaurant of the era, at the Windsor Arms hotel in Toronto. Molinaro, Corinne McLuhan and Toye, eds., *Letters*, 537.

audience research or public relations or simply espionage. It is sometimes called "data processing". On the other hand, apropos money, it was long ago obsolesced by "credit" whose natural tendency is towards debt and poverty. When given the speed of the computer, the credit card covers a lot of ground.

The main verb in all this is the speed of light, which also alters the role of politician from a party representative to a charismatic image. This image obsolesces parties and policies alike. This is very compressed, but I know you are busy – perhaps not too busy to hear a joke that has just turned up. It concerns a traveler returning from the U.K. with a dozen bottles of whiskey. At the Customs he is asked: "What have you got here?" He replies: "Holy water." The Customs officer opens one of the bottles and takes a swig, and says: "That's not holy water – that's whiskey!" At this the traveler exclaimed rapturously: "It's a miracle!"

Corinne and I pray that your Christmas and New Year will be liberally strewn with miracles!

[M.M.]

December 21, 1977

Dear Pierre:

I enclose a jest that I hope will turn the Separatist tide!

Again, a Blessed New Year for you, and for Canada, and the world.

[M.M.]

The jest:

One day Trudeau had an inspiration and called Lucifer on the phone, and found that Lucifer could speak eloquent French. They talked for a long time and Lucifer had some superb ideas and suggestions. After the call, Trudeau checked on the charges, since he didn't wish it to appear as a bill to be paid by the party, and was told the cost was $175.00. He said: "Very good. I got wonderful value for my money on that call." When Levesque heard about the call, he, too, put in his call and had a long talk with Lucifer. At the end of the call he asked for the charges, since he didn't wish it to appear as a public charge. He was told: "No charge." "But", says he, "you charged Trudeau $175.00." The answer then came: "Yes, sir, but his was a long distance call, and yours is local!"

1978

In the year 1978, there was little apparent contact between McLuhan and Trudeau. The prime minister was trying to manage the national effects of the Parti Québécois win which, among other things, emboldened other provinces to ask for more rights. The previous summer, he had established a task force on Canadian unity.

June 19, 1978.

Dear Marshall,

Thank you for your letter of May 23 and the enclosed documentation.

As always, I find your thoughts most interesting. Your comments* on an existing biculturalism in our school system present a new slant on the reasons behind the growing problem of dyslexia. I am pleased that you and Arthur Hurst are to receive funding from the Ontario government to pursue this research.[193]

I was interested to read your essay on Quebec and English Canada in its final draft. In the light of recent events, your theories take on a prophetic aspect. Camille Laurin's White Paper on Culture would seem to bear out some of your premises. Future events will no doubt prove or disprove their validity. Perhaps you and I will have the opportunity to discuss this at some time.

*They also explain for me my sometime bewilderment at the lack of logic of many in the T.V. generation!

[P.E.T.]

---

193 Government funding for Hurst's stereoscopic head camera never actually came through. Marchand, *McLuhan*, 301 n. 59.

10th November, 1978

Dear Pierre:

Imagine my discomfiture when I discovered that October 18th had flitted past without a birthday greeting to you!

In place of a birthday greeting, a couple of one-liners that may come in handy:

Time wounds all heels.

Apropos the new Pope[194]:

We used to have a Peter's Pence, and now we have a Poll Tax.

Whereas the Church was thought to have been built on a rock, it is now built on a pole.

The inflation situation is world-wide, yet it demands a scapegoat for each region. As for unemployment, the nature of work necessarily changes in an information environment based on electric speed, so that what used to be called espionage now appears to be a natural form of human occupation.[195]

You may find some use for my definition of "charisma", namely "Looking like a lot of other people." Cronkite[196] looks like everybody's favourite guardian, and Carter looks like the All-American Southern boy, namely Huck Finn.

We keep up our prayers for you and other crucial figures.

[M.M.]

194 The Polish cardinal Karol Józef Wojtyla had been elected Pope John Paul II on October 16, 1978, and served until his death on April 2, 2005.

195 Someone has added, in handwriting, "and the largest!"

196 Walter Cronkite, often called the most trusted television news anchor and reporter of the 1960s and 1970s.

6th December, 1978

Dear Pierre:

Seeing a headline about the "Unity Task Force", I was suddenly struck by the incongruity of relating bilingualism to unity. If all Canadians spoke both languages there would be great enrichment of our culture, but there would be a much greater tendency towards plurality and diversity rather than unity. Surely to reach unity as a desired effect of a bilingualism programme requires imposition from above. On the other hand a bilingual pattern could be <u>acceptable</u> if it grew up naturally from below. But again, such an idea would lead not to unity, but rather to diversity. Somehow a non sequitur has entered the rationale of the bilingualism programme. The federal idea of free association is not the same thing as unity. Do not English Canadians speak American and feel at home in the U.S.A. without the slightest thought of unity? Many French Canadians must likewise feel quite at home in English Canada linguistically without supposing that they have any commitment to unity. I am trying to discover the line of reasoning that led to the adoption of a bilingualism policy as a means of unity, when it almost certainly has the opposite effect.

Just as a possible parallel, Governor Brown in California was originally flatly opposed to Proposition 13,[197] but managed to switch horses in midstream and to take on Number 13 as his personal policy and as his primary election issue. This switch proved to be completely successful. In other words, might it not be entirely practical to modulate the bilingual programme as a means of fostering enrichment rather than unity?

[M.M.]

197 California Proposition 13 (People's Initiative to Limit Property Taxation), passed earlier that year, placed extreme limitations on property tax increases.

December 15, 1978

Dear Marshall:

Many thanks for your kind note of November 10.

Please don't feel too wretched. I was not entirely forgotten by your family on the occasion of my birthday![198]

With kindest regards and wishes.

Sincerely,
Pierre[199]

December 18, 1978

Dear Marshall,

Thank you for your letter of December 6 in which you comment on bilingualism as it relates to national unity.

On April 1, 2013, the Inuktitut language joined English and French as an official language of the territory of Nunavut.

I am not quite certain what reasoning lies behind your statement that if all Canadians were bilingual, there would be more diversity in the country. Surely if we could all communicate with each other, we would feel a greater degree of unity. You say that we feel no unity with Americans even though we speak the same language. This may be true to some extent; however, I think we feel closer to Americans than we do to others and that this feeling has resulted not just from geographic proximity but also the idea that they are less "foreign" than those who do not speak one of our languages.

198 Trudeau was friends with two of McLuhan's daughters.

199 Trudeau wrote a note across the bottom of the page: "For your collection, here is a great one-liner from Chateaubriand: 'Il y a des jours où il faut dépenser son mépris avec économie, à cause du grand nombre de nècessiteux.'" Trudeau must have been quoting from memory, as the actual quotation is "Il y a des temps où l'on ne doit dépenser le mépris qu'avec l'économie, à cause du grand nombre de nécessiteux."

As for your assertion that the government's bilingual policy is divisive, I fear that you, as well as a great many other Canadians, have not fully understood the purpose of the policy. The Official Languages Act guaranteed that Canadians could deal with their federal government in the official language of their choice. The main thrust of the law was not to change the languages spoken, or to make people bilingual, but rather to ensure that both[200] the principal languages of the country would be fully respected at the federal level. The promotion of this concept of language equality in turn ensures that the linguistic groups are treated equally by their government. Neither group will feel that the other is being shown favoritism by the government. When people are made to feel inferior or unfairly treated on the grounds of the language they speak, it is impossible that they feel any kindred spirit with the group they see as being treated as superior. In this way, the language policy does promote unity. This is the line of reasoning that led to the adoption of the policy and its implementation.

I hope that I have explained this to your satisfaction, Marshall, and thank you again for giving me the benefit of your views.

With kind personal regards and prayers.

Yours sincerely,
Pierre

200 Underlined in blue ink, likely by Trudeau.

1979

1st February, 1979

Dear Pierre:

Your thoughtful reply to my query about what line of thinking lay behind the bilingual policy brought to my mind the familiar phrase of Baudelaire[201] in his Envoi to Les Fleurs du Mal, "Hypocrite lecteur, mon semblable, mon frère". The "lecteur" is the reader of the poem who "puts it on" as a mask through which he looks at the world. (The hypocrite is a mask-wearer.) When the reader "puts on" the poem he inevitably distorts it, and this is reciprocated by the poet, who "puts on" the reader as his "semblable" and his "frère". The poet has a natural grievance against the reader's distortion of his poem, and so he enjoys the activity of distorting the reader in turn by putting on the reader as his mask. (Behind the idea of the "put-on" is the metaphysical idea of the cognitive agent who is and becomes the thing known in classical philosophy.)

If a poem has the natural and inevitable power of altering both the reader and the poet and their inter-relationship, how much more is this true of our two languages! The speaker of any language assumes it as a medium or a mask by which he experiences the world in a special way, and by which he relates to people in a very special way. The French tongue as a mask or medium at the federal level has a quite different meaning and function from the same tongue at the private level. A language in the hands of a lawyer or a judge or a bureaucrat has a quite different significance from the same language used by friends or enemies. I suggest that your approach to bilingualism as a means of "language equality" is abstract and objective, but not related to the

201 French poet Charles Pierre Baudelaire (1821–1867).

experiential, subjective level. That is not to say this is a misguided attitude, but it merely indicates that the effects of languages as media are quite different from the input or intended meanings. All inputs have side effects which are usually considered irrelevant by the speaker or sender.

You are probably familiar with the Shannon-Weaver model of communication theory. (I enclose a copy of it in an article on the two hemispheres of the brain.) Shannon and Weaver were mathematicians who considered the side effects as noise. They assumed that these could be eliminated by simply stepping up the charge of energy in the circuit.

The left hemisphere, the one developed in our Western world by phonetic literacy, is the lineal and visual mode of objective awareness, whereas the right hemisphere is the acoustic and involved mode of awareness. The third world is almost entirely right hemisphere, and the first world is tending, under electric information environments, to transform itself into a new kind of third world. The third world, on the other hand, is frantically trying to develop the attributes of the left hemisphere by lineal and quantitative education and production. The confusion and loss of identity in the first world is one of the results we experience as we acquire third world characteristics (loss of private identity and loss of goals, etc.). Should China be effective in acquiring phonetic western literacy, the explosion in that ancient culture would be total. The ancient Greeks did not long survive their own acquisition of phonetic literacy. The explosion within our own world is telling enough and is the occasion for much prayer from us for you and your great responsibility.

Corinne and I thought that the Christmas card photo of you and the boys was and is most eloquent and delightful.

[M.M.]

16th April, 1979

On March 26, Trudeau had called for a May 22 federal election. He held onto his own seat, but his government was defeated, resulting in a minority government under the Progressive Conservatives, led by Joe Clark.

Dear Pierre:

I have been following the election campaign and wish to make a brief note, namely that since the issues are tending to get "hot", it would be a huge advantage to shift the main broadcast coverage to radio. Radio is a "hot" medium and is indispensable when the issues get hot. TV is a fantasy medium, and has good reason to be called "cool" or all-involving. The current issue of Business Week, I have been told, carries comments on the surprise return of Bill Clement as Governor of Texas, the first Republican in many years. He did it by radio – radio spots. The best man in the world for such spot coverage is my friend Tony Schwartz in New York City. He put Carter in by some inspired spots at the last moment. Tony is basically a sound, or radio man, although he has a little book on television called The Responsive Chord. I tried to get in touch with Bill Coutts[202] about this but failed to reach him.

Radio charisma is a completely different thing from TV charisma. TV charisma means looking like a lot of nice people, e.g. the Cronkite image. Radio charisma merely consists in sounding dedicated.

Address for Tony Schwartz is:
455 West 56th St.,
NEW YORK, N.Y. 10019
U.S.A.

[M.M.]

202 McLuhan meant James Coutts (1938–2013), Trudeau's principal secretary at the time. Molinaro, Corinne McLuhan and Toye, eds., *Letters*, 544. I made contact with Coutts to arrange an interview, but he died before we could meet.

July 25, 1979.

Dear Marshall,[203]

I have just reread the telegram which you sent to me the day after the election.

It is indeed time for renewal and I find it most encouraging that there is so much good will and determination by so many who want to take part in the refreshment process.

With many warm thanks and wishes.

Sincerely, and God bless!
Pierre

7th September, 1979

Dear Pierre:

I think there is no question but that your beard has cooled your image many degrees! There may be a time when you would wish to hot it up again. This, by the way, reminds me of a factor that relates to our Centre here: we have a monopoly on the study of the effects of media and technology. I wish this were not so but the monopoly is very real. The Greeks did not even study the effects of the alphabet on themselves, or its relation to the rise of Euclid and rationalism.

Both the beard and the Centre show up in a YouTube audio clip of an interview with Trudeau by a former head of the university's McLuhan program.

https://www.youtube.com/watch?v=1K4LooUizml

Another matter is that this is the last year for the Centre as it is presently related to the University of Toronto. This is mainly a financial matter, although there is also the fact that they cannot find anybody to replace me. I personally know of some possible replacements and this

203 This letter was on stationery with the letterhead "Leader of the Opposition – Chef de L'Opposition," as it was written during Trudeau's brief tenure in that office.

could be one of the matters I would like to discuss with you when we get together.

Our own study of the relations of media and politics might be an aspect that would favour some support. Hutchins[204] once set up a Center for the Study of Democratic Institutions in California, which is still functioning. It would be easy to improve on their programme. There is, incidentally, a basic reason why we have this monopoly on the study of the effects of media and I would be happy to discuss that with you also when we get together.

Jimmy Carter, by the way, is the first American President from the Deep South,[205] and many of his problems arise from a culture-clash between his oral tradition and the bureaucratic world of modern politics and government. I have often said that he is, as it were, Huck Finn in the White House. Since he is coming up here in November it might be feasible to be of some help to him![206]

[M.M.]

The meeting with Trudeau may have taken place, but the meeting with Carter did not: McLuhan suffered a massive stroke on September 26, leaving him almost totally unable to communicate normally.

On November 21, Trudeau retired. His decision held for a little less than a month, as the Progressive Conservative government, under Prime Minister Clark, was defeated on a budget vote and an election was called for February 18, 1980. The Liberals had not yet chosen a new leader and Trudeau was ready to come back. They won a majority.

With McLuhan no longer able to head up his Centre, the university decided to shut it down and instead offer a program in McLuhan's name. Even a letter of support from the prime minister did not change the decision.

Marchand, *Marshall McLuhan*, 284.

204 Educator Robert Maynard Hutchins.

205 Arguably, the first president from the Deep South was Andrew Jackson, born in the Waxhaws area on the border of North and South Carolina and buried in Tennessee. He served from 1829 to 1837.

206 The next piece of correspondence is an October 18, 1979, birthday card from McLuhan to Trudeau, with "Happy Birthday" written across the top and signed "All the best, Marshall" (in handwriting that is not his, a month after his stroke). It was not sent to the prime minister at his official residence, but to "Monsieur Pierre Trudeau" at 541 Acacia in Ottawa.

1980

April 28, 1980.

Dear Marshall,

I have been hearing about the difficulties you are presently experiencing at the Centre and would like you to know that you are in my thoughts. You had intimated that there were financial problems, but I had no idea that the University was considering closing the Centre.

Who knows better than you and I the bitter irony of the old saw about a prophet in his own land... However, you can be assured of a prominent place not only in Canadian history, but in the annals of technocracy. It is heartening to see that the press is treating you with the respect you are owed.

All the best to you and Corinne.

Yours sincerely, and God bless,
Pierre[207]

In 2017, McLuhan's library, housed at the University of Toronto, and his personal archives at Library and Archives Canada were honoured with a place in UNESCO's Memory of the World register. The United Nations agency works for global cooperation in the areas of education, science, culture and communications.

https://www.utoronto.ca/news/famed-u-t-professor-marshall-mcluhan-s-library-given-united-nations-heritage-designation

207 I've seen reference to a December 1980 Christmas card from Trudeau to McLuhan, but have not been able to locate it.

1981

[Lake][208]
January 7, 1981.
(Ottawa, K1A 0A2)

My dear Corinne,

It is with great sadness that I write to express my sympathy to you and your family. Despite the setback which Marshall suffered more than a year ago, the news of his death was still a terrible shock.

Much will be said and written, and rightly so, about his marvelous intellect, his years of teaching, his global eminence as a social theorist, as a seminal scholar and writer. But the dominant thoughts in my own mind are of you and your children, and of my own sense of loss.

I have longed valued his friendship, and have warm memories of our stimulating conversations. His letters were a constant delight, even when they included those terrible puns he used to urge me to use in political debate.

Marshall's life and work increased my sense of pride in being a Canadian. His crackling mind provided me with much pleasure and many lasting insights. His work, I am sure, will live on to challenge thoughtful men and women of future generations.

At this time, perhaps what is of most consolation to you is your knowledge of his great faith, and of the goodness of his life. He was a man whose fame did not dilute his profound awareness that our destiny in life is to love and to serve.

208 Trudeau has corrected this by hand to show he is not actually in Ottawa. It looks more like "Lahr" than "Lake," but writing from his retreat at Harrington Lake makes more sense than Germany.

In the name of the government and people of Canada, I want to express the sympathy of a nation which is saddened by his death, and grateful for his life. For my part, I simply pray that God will grant strength, lasting peace and serenity of spirit to you and your family.

Yours sincerely,
Pierre

Resonating

I don't know how history will ultimately judge Pierre Trudeau as a politician, and I don't care. He is the standard by which I measure all national leaders: smart, inquisitive, worldly, articulate, passionate about his own country, open to other cultures, charismatic in a way that is not dangerous.

Canadians who still struggle with questions of national identity, that deeply ingrained national pastime, should remember Trudeau's remarks to the House of Commons in October 1971, and the rest of the world should pay attention:

> A policy of multiculturalism within a bilingual framework commends itself to the government as the most suitable means of assuring the cultural freedom of Canadians. Such a policy should help to break down discriminatory attitudes and cultural jealousies. National unity if it is to mean anything in the deeply personal sense, must be founded on confidence in one's own individual identity; out of this can grow respect for that of others and a willingness to share ideas, attitudes and assumptions. A vigorous policy of multiculturalism will help create this initial confidence. It can form the base of a society which is based on fair play for all.[209]

These ideas have infused my own for over 40 years, as have many of McLuhan's. My thoughts turned often to his interface and resonant interval, which were foundations of my own cutting-edge journalism on

209 Trudeau, *Conversation with Canadians*, 32.

multiculturalism, trying to teach others why we must understand those we live with in the global village. I didn't know McLuhan had become generally unknown until, trying to finish up my graduate degree in liberal studies at Rutgers University in 2007, I failed to find a professor to supervise my thesis if McLuhan were the topic (my first course in liberal studies, "The Great Courts of Europe," was, if not global, at least international, and I wrote a small essay about portraits, their own kind of communications media, across several centuries).

I switched programs, from liberal studies to global affairs, got my master's degree, continued into the doctoral program. I settled on a dissertation topic, one I'd already begun to explore in a feminist methodology course: an analysis of the ways in which the immigrant experience has been affected by the wired globe. And then I decided to attend McLuhan100 Then Now Next, an international conference at the University of Toronto in November 2011, one of many events worldwide held that year to mark the centenary of McLuhan's birth. I figured I would put my interest in McLuhan to rest.

Instead, eavesdropping during a gap between sessions, I overheard York University professor B.W. Powe tell a colleague that the Trudeau-McLuhan correspondence had not been studied, and I changed dissertation topics. I hadn't known McLuhan and Trudeau were friends, and it never occurred to me that just the existence of this correspondence was not in itself valuable – the medium being, after all, the message. But, of course, the value of the correspondence goes beyond the mere fact of it or even the glimpse it gives into the relationship between two of the most influential Canadians of the twentieth century, both in Canada and globally. Their discussions remain fresh, whether about privacy issues under new media realities, identity politics and violence, the changing realities of the working world or the manipulation of media images. The Trudeau-McLuhan correspondence is a unique conversation about Canada's place in the world and about using media politically.

Economic globalization is often considered in isolation from other forms of globalization, such as the cultural or environmental, unthinkingly demonizing globalization entirely. I think neither McLuhan nor Trudeau, a trained economist, saw globalization primarily, let alone exclusively, through the lens of economics. Just as important, and unlike many people today, including some world leaders, they didn't delude themselves into seeing no connection between globalized money and globalizing culture and technology. They had a nuanced understanding that did not simply pit the national against the international, although McLuhan pointed out the urge of financial leaders to try to convince otherwise. The business community, even while conglomerating, "demands a 'double standard,'" McLuhan wrote to Trudeau on November 3, 1968. "While making rapid adjustments to changing technologies, it expects the educational and political establishments to remain rigidly fixed in the old pattern." I find that the most positive take on global affairs is often found in the business section of the newspaper, because it values nation less than money.

I often view globalization through the tighter focus of glocalization,[210] shaped by a lifelong interest in the meshing and meetings of cultures and culture in all possible ways. Once that is how you focus on the world, examples are everywhere:

- Global fast-food conglomerates have recognized the need to adapt their regimented preparations to local tastes if they wish to succeed in a country other than the one in which they were born.[211] Firms know that their core competencies give them only a limited competitive advantage "unless their production is sensitive to the demands of consumers, and the shifting cultural context in which they operate."[212]
- The world's highest award in architecture was awarded in 2017 to a trio of young people, cited for being "a local firm in an increasingly globalized world."

> "They help us to see, in a most beautiful and poetic way, that the answer to the question is not 'either/or' and that

210 "[A] complex interaction of the global and local characterized by cultural borrowing." Manfred B. Steger, *Globalism: Market Ideology Meets Terrorism* (2nd ed.). Lanham, MD: Rowman & Littlefield, 2005, 40.

211 For an account of Taco Bell's efforts to meet the tastes of consumers in China, see https://www.nytimes.com/2017/02/10/business/china-kfc-taco-bell.html.

212 Robert O'Brien and Marc Williams, *Global Political Economy: Evolution and Dynamics*. London: Palgrave MacMillan, 2004, 185.

> we can, at least in architecture, aspire to have both," [the Pritzker award jury] continued, "our roots firmly in place and our arms outstretched to the rest of the world."[213]

- The Internet itself is glocal, though no longer unrestricted, as it was originally, "born as a world without borders, developed to withstand a nuclear war and allow the surviving individuals to communicate."[214] It's bizarre, all things considered, but CBC-TV doesn't allow its programs to be streamed across the U.S. border, so I couldn't watch the Leonard Cohen memorial concert broadcast in November 2017.

When trying to understand any relationship, one faces the question not only of attraction but of influence. McLuhan cited Trudeau in his work; Trudeau was "a fan of McLuhan."[215] The Trudeau-McLuhan relationship, one of mutual admiration, undoubtedly had its moments in which one inspired the other, but did these two strong intellects influence each other? The answer cannot be that linear, a matter of going from point A to point B. Influence is cumulative, often unconscious – perhaps at its best, "labyrinthine,"[216] an insight that seems particularly apt when considering McLuhan. They had an interface, there were gaps, there were resonating intervals.

Although I have not been able to pinpoint the date on which Trudeau and McLuhan first became aware of each other, I do know when I became aware of them myself. I was in grade 10 when Trudeau became prime minister in 1968 and Trudeaumania infected so many Canadians. A lot of us were still on a post-Expo high. I was probably still excited that we finally had our own flag and many of us were thrilled too that, unexpectedly, we'd found our JFK. For some Canadians, national identity itself was entwined with Trudeau:

213 https://www.nytimes.com/2017/03/01/arts/design/3-win-the-pritzker-long-a-prize-for-starchitects.html

214 Richard Langhorne, *The Coming of Globalization: Its Evolution and Contemporary Consequences*. New York: Palgrave, 2001, 10.

215 Alec Scott, "Marshall's Laws." *UofT Magazine* 39:1 (Autumn 2011): 26–31, at 30.

216 Harold Bloom, *The Anatomy of Influence: Literature as a Way of Life*. New Haven: Yale University Press, 2011, 26.

> The astonishing and sudden victory of Trudeau, with his historically unprecedented – for Canada, anyway – understanding of politics as public spectacle, and his savvy suturing of persona with policy, is at least partly accounted for by the shift in the national imagination made possible by 1967. Distinctive as he was, and remains, his arrival was also perfectly timed. As Larry Zolf noted in 1984, "Trudeau was our permanent Expo."[217]

Following the example of my history teacher, who said Trudeau was really special, I fell under the influence too. My first newspaper article, published in April 1968 in my hometown paper, the *Oshawa Times*, was about the political convention (which I did not attend) at which he became Liberal leader. During the federal election campaign that June, I went with my best friend to the local shopping centre to catch a glimpse of Trudeau at a campaign event. I stuffed envelopes for our local Liberal candidate; the candidate lost, but the campaign poster is taped to a door in my office (didn't plan it that way, but a Leonard Cohen poster is taped to the other door – well, the two of them were good friends). Trudeau's autograph, framed, hangs by my desk; my father asked the then-retired Trudeau for it for me at the 1990 Liberal leadership convention in Calgary, which saw Jean Chrétien become leader. On a drive back from Montreal to New Jersey in 2003, my husband and I made a detour to St-Rémi-de-Napierville to visit Trudeau's gravesite.

Part of what made Trudeau special was his exceptional command of English. Exchange programs between high school students in Quebec and other parts of Canada were popular in the 1960s, and here was a leader who embodied those programs' goals of understanding across the nation's founding cultures and beyond.

> In 1968, with the exception of Trudeau and Paul Martin Sr., attempts at French by candidates for the Liberal leadership

217 Pevere and Dymond, *Mondo Canuck*, 220–221. Trudeau is the only politician given his own chapter in this pop history, because the authors consider him "the greatest media star" Canada ever produced.

> were an embarrassment, not least because nobody seemed to care how badly he spoke.[218]

Well, I cared. A Canadian prime minister who isn't fluent in both languages really is an embarrassment. And the situation has changed:

> That indifference did not last long. Among most of the candidates for the Liberal leadership in 2013, French was far from perfect but it was not embarrassing.
>
> That change had its roots in the early years of the Trudeau government. Almost by stealth the capacity to speak French became a step up the ladder of power, whether in the cabinet, the courts or the ranks of the public service.[219]

Those of us who view issues from a global perspective must always keep in mind that all languages, having their own vocabularies and coming out of their own cultures, will bring necessary nuances to the table.

On March 23, 1970, while researching my grade 12 media project, I met McLuhan briefly at his Centre. I was tagging along for the day with *Toronto Star* columnist Lotta Dempsey,[220] who was there to interview McLuhan's associate, Harley Parker.

"I noticed a tall greying man in a grey suit in the next room," I wrote later in my rather cloying, youthfully arrogant, report:

> He was so nondescript that I knew he had to be Marshall McLuhan. He was. Hearing I was doing a project on communications, he said, "I think you should make a *camera obscura*," which he then translated into English, not trusting my status as a Latin scholar, and explained. I don't remember listening – I was too stunned!

218 https://www.cbc.ca/news/politics/the-2-trudeaus-and-the-lesson-of-1968-1.1371425. Martin's son, Paul Martin Jr., also a Liberal, was prime minister from December 2003 to February 2006.

219 http://www.cbc.ca/news/politics/the-2-trudeaus-and-the-lesson-of-1968-1.1371425

220 Lotta Dempsey, "Elaine meets the newsmakers." *Toronto Star* (undated article, likely June 1970, from my own files).

I do remember McLuhan explaining why the fishnet stockings popular at the time were more involving – I don't remember him saying "sexier" – than regular nylons, because one had to mentally fill in the spaces. He had written about this earlier, but it was all new to me.

"The gap is where the action is," McLuhan said that day, a phrase he used often in his work and letters, including one to Trudeau. "The generation gap generates change."

Several years later, as an English lit major at U of T's University College, when I was seriously grappling for the first time with belief in God, it was the gap, the interface, the resonating interval, that I fell back on. God, I decided, was the filling responsible for the action in gaps and at interfaces that I could explain no other way.

I don't know why I didn't study with McLuhan during my U of T years. Probably I was intimidated, despite the natural fit with my own interests. McLuhan's seminars were "the dawn of interdisciplinarity," according to Dominique Scheffel-Dunand, former director of the McLuhan Coach House Institute. "'He pioneered the concept.'"[221] I was attracted to journalism as a career because I didn't want to specialize. I didn't realize at the time that my aversion to work specialization placed me firmly within McLuhan's analysis of the way roles in my generation were developing.

There are frustrating gaps in the Trudeau-McLuhan correspondence. Despite references to Trudeau's marriage, there are none for the births of his children and no direct mention of his divorce. Although I have been told by several excellent sources that Trudeau often visited the McLuhan home, the letters are silent on this point too.

A more serious gap, for a study of matters both Canadian and global, occurs in the letters for 1970. I have seen no direct correspondence between the two men that year until after the October Crisis, and only four pieces for 1970 altogether, two of them from McLuhan to Jim Davey.

The October Crisis involved domestic terrorists and Trudeau's invocation of the federal War Measures Act, the first time the law

221 Scott, "Marshall's Laws," 29.

had been invoked in peacetime.[222] One of the events precipitating the crisis – the kidnapping of British trade commissioner James Richard Cross – made Canada "the first Western nation to experience a political kidnapping at home."[223] Davey was intensely involved in the handling of the crisis, directing "the Strategic Operations Centre that devised the federal government's response,"[224] and his involvement continued once the immediate crisis passed. I cannot believe McLuhan held back from giving Trudeau advice, solicited or not, during this period.

When McLuhan wrote about the global village, he wasn't talking about a village of global migrants – traditionally, a village is a place one thinks of as stable, unlike large urban centres. One of his critics has claimed that "global city" would better capture McLuhan's notion of an agitated fragmented web.[225] (Trudeau took a more optimistic view, writing to McLuhan on March 17, 1975, that "this tension can be turned into a most creative force, so that the 'global village' will gradually take shape as a true city, i.e., a place worth living for all mankind. Please go on helping us to keep on the alert!") More disconcerting to me, because it seemed to undermine the gravity of the concept, I overheard someone at the centenary conference in Toronto in 2011 say McLuhan himself ultimately switched from "global village" to "global theatre." But I have come to understand that the price of tackling McLuhan is accepting that he constantly played with his work and his readers as part of a performance. (He is known to have said that all of his work was satire.[226]) McLuhan used "global theatre" a couple of times in his correspondence with Trudeau, and I appreciate the concision of his perception that "Homogeneity, the old idea of nation, is useless in the global theatre of gaps and interfaces."[227]

222 At the time, Alan Borovoy, executive director of the Toronto Civil Liberties Union, said on CBC-TV that he "had no idea that the War Measures Act was still on the statute books." Cook, *Teeth of Time*, 100.

223 Ronald D. Crelinsten and Alex P. Schmid. "Western Responses to Terrorism: A Twenty-Five Year Balance Sheet. *Terrorism and Political Violence* 4:4 (1992): 307–340, at 309.

224 Cook, *Teeth of Time*, 117.

225 Hedley Bull, *The Anarchical Society: A Study of Order in World Politics* (3rd ed.). New York: Columbia University Press, 1977, 263.

226 De Kerckhove [McLuhan100].

227 McLuhan, *Culture*, 170.

For me, the global village has always been real, even while I can acknowledge from my advantage point that most people, while technically part of that village, are too poor or powerless to be in control of their connection to it. As an immigrant to the United States and the child of a second-generation Canadian-born mother and a father who fled Nazi Germany, I am almost inherently interested in not only compromise and consolidation, but also understanding and managing life across borders or boundaries. This is also the greatest gift my refugee grandmother, Carola Kahn, gave me: the gift of maintaining connections, which, from childhood, I understood as not only a pleasant pastime but critical to one's emotional – and, sometimes, actual physical – well-being.

"An immigrant was a man between two worlds; so two places shaped every immigrant experience."[228] Immigrants also shape their destinations. Each individual is a weaving of identities and attachments, and this may be the fundamental challenge to developing successful immigration projects. After all, "if geographical location was the single determining factor, then the moment an individual emigrated from one country to another, he or she would immediately be indistinguishable from others in that country."[229] That insight should give us pause and give us empathy.

Although we see borders on maps as lines and although we know about border controls such as fences and visualize them too as lines, borders are really border zones, somewhat fluid, definitely fuzzy, with influences flowing more than one way. Historically, there has been limited political usefulness to geographically logical borders, those using natural markers such as rivers or mountain ranges; when the power exists, they can be breached. As actually lived, borders are often borderlands, an interface where disparate things meet and react. For most of human history, the movement of people came to mark the borders of governed entities; borders did not originate to keep people within

228 Robert Harney and Harold Troper. *Immigrants: A Portrait of the Urban Experience, 1890–1930.* Toronto: Van Nostrand Reinhold, 1975, 1.

229 Roy J. Eidelson and Ian S. Lustick, "National Identity Repertoires, Territory and Globalization," in Mabel Berezin and Martin Schain (eds.), *Europe Without Borders: Remapping Territory, Citizenship and Identity in a Transnational Age*. Baltimore: Johns Hopkins University Press, 89–117, at 91.

those entities. When it comes to the global climate crisis, borders have no effective meaning at all.

I had an immediate understanding of the networking and webbing I learned about in my global affairs studies and tied a number of my essays to the global village, citing McLuhan even in my political economics paper:

> We can now live, not just amphibiously in divided and distinguished worlds, but pluralistically in many worlds and culture simultaneously. We are no more committed to one culture – to a single ratio among the human senses – any more than to one book or to one language or to one technology… What began as a "Romantic" reaction towards organic wholeness may or may not have hastened the discovery of electro-magnetic waves. But certainly the electro-magnetic discoveries have recreated the simultaneous "field" in all human affairs so that the human family now exists under conditions of a "global village."[230]

The webbing is everywhere. While working with the Trudeau-McLuhan letters, I learned, serendipitously, that Johanna "Hanchen" Marx, paternal grandmother of the Marx Brothers, was born in the same German town where my father's family had lived for centuries, in a house owned by one of my ancestors. McLuhan mentions the Marx Brothers to Davey in an August 27, 1969, letter.

During my first stint living in the United States, in the late 1970s and not yet a citizen, I was aggressively Canadian both in the books I chose to display in our apartment and in my pre-emptive defence of a country my new American friends knew nothing about, aside from recognizing Pierre and Margaret from tabloid photos and having a fear of Quebec separation that seemed overblown and shallow and which I did not share. By now, though, I do share Trudeau and McLuhan's concerns about the dangers of unthinking nationalism and, often, nationalism's irrelevance. Playing off the title of what is arguably Trudeau's most known essay, "La Nouvelle Trahison des Clercs," found in English

230 McLuhan, *Gutenberg Galaxy*, 31.

translation as "New Treason of the Intellectuals" in his *Federalism and the French Canadians*, McLuhan wrote that "Pierre Trudeau points to the new treason of the literati: 'It is not the concept of nation that is retrograde; it is the idea that the nation must necessarily be sovereign.'"[231]

In those days, as soon as I crossed the border from Canada into the US, usually by car, I was cut off from Canadian news – not even US border cities like Watertown, NY, carried Canadian newspapers. Maybe, if I were lucky, I'd be able to pick up scratchy weak CBC radio signals on an election night. The most exciting moment of my first visit to Boston was finding a copy of *Maclean's* magazine for sale in Harvard Square.

As an immigrant today, my world is often virtual. I can get most of the news online, I can video-chat with family and friends, and international phone rates have dropped precipitously. I can tour my old neighbourhoods online and walk virtually past the house in which I grew up. (I note that physical travel to and from Canada has not undergone the same improvements, whether by car or air.) Back in the late '70s, I remember being furious with the owner of the excellent bookstore in my New York City neighbourhood when I asked why, despite stocking much European fiction in translation, she had no Canadian titles, and being told that, if there were Canadian writers who were any good, she'd stock them. (Another American who did not understand the links between global economic forces – this time in the publishing world – and global culture!) Now I order online.

I am now also a dual citizen – more of a challenge for a Canadian in a post-9/11 world than I'd assumed. When I applied for US citizenship, someone at an early stage of paperwork mistyped my surname as "Khan" and, ever since, I've run into problems with official documents, even when renewing the Canadian passport I've had since I was 16. I'm angry for myself, but also for all those Khans who apparently now fall under immediate suspicion.

I now think even more deeply about citizenship rights and obligations, borderlands, and what Ayelet Shachar calls, in her eponymous 2009 book, "the birthright lottery." Other models that have been tossed

231 McLuhan, *Culture*, 170.

around include "new citizenship," which is essentially economic and social; post-national political citizenship, based on human rights principles; or rethinking national citizenship altogether.[232] It is also tantalizing to think of the nation state itself as a kind of border, a space in which national particularism or the ethnic dimensions of each historic state are reconciled with the universal claims of citizenship.[233] Though perhaps that is naïve.

I haven't read the online speculations about what McLuhan might make of President Donald Trump, who "is no longer just the message. In many cases, he has become the medium, the ether through which all other stories flow."[234] I speculate on my own: what would the truly devout Trudeau and McLuhan make of the 21st-century global village, its leaders, its media? They were not innocents and they were not perfect, but they were civilized as well as globalized and they matter.

Canada, however, remains a global afterthought and as little a part of the American consciousness as ever, although, as recent years have shown, "sometimes the worst thing to happen to a country can be American attention."[235] When Trump met Prime Minister Justin Trudeau in Washington in February 2017, and a reporter asked whether he "had ever visited Canada, presidential aides cut the photo op short and escorted the media out."[236]

There was, however, another photo present when the two leaders met, a gift from Trudeau to Trump. It is an image from an earlier era, an image that smashes borders of time and place and, in its meanings, pits the inspirational global against the ignorant parochial, with the former victorious. The photo is of Pierre Trudeau, a head-table guest at a November 5, 1981, dinner at the Waldorf-Astoria in Manhattan, and Trump, speaking at the lectern. In the photo, Trump is looking at the larger audience, not at Pierre. The prime minister is staring into

232 Dominique Schnapper, "The European Debate on Citizenship," *Daedalus* 126:3 (1997): 199–222, at 203.

233 Dominique Schnapper, "Citizenship and National Identity in Europe," *Nations and Nationalism* 8:1 (2002): 1–14, at 6.

234 https://www.nytimes.com/2017/02/22/technology/trump-news-media-ignore.html?_r=0

235 http://www.bbc.com/news/world-us-canada-36512850

236 http://license.icopyright.net/user/viewFreeUse.act?fuid=MjQ3MTMyOTI%3D

space or at the dinnerware, but not at Trump, and his left hand appears to be gloved in leather.

Trudeau was being honoured that night for fighting for human progress, by the Society of the Family of Man, an interfaith society founded in 1963 by the Council of Churches of the City of New York. Previous recipients included JFK and Lester Pearson.[237] In his remarks, he

> appealed to countries to work together...[and] devote resources to those in need...
>
> Trudeau warned that the world is standing "at the narrowing corridor of opportunity... the longer we delay action on pressing global problems, the less opportunity we will have to avoid the potentially disastrous collisions ahead."[238]

McLuhan's "collide-oscope of interfaced situations"[239] and Trudeau's words about misguided dangerous nationalism – "Open the frontiers, this people is dying of asphyxiation"[240] – are only two of the messages from the past brought sharply to mind through the medium of that photo, for reasons both old and disturbingly contemporary.

For me, Trudeau and McLuhan never get old and, in the following excerpt from a 1999 magazine article, I hear both their voices, resonating into a better future:

> Prime Minister Pierre Trudeau aggressively promoted the idea of a national culture constituted by its cultural pluralism. He argued that: "Uniformity is neither desirable nor possible in a country the size of Canada. We should not even be able to agree upon the kind of Canadian to choose as a model, let alone persuade most people to emulate it." To those who argue that multiculturalism is a dangerous recipe for a fractiously decentralized state, Trudeau's response was to make a virtue of the paradox. In 1970, to the Annual

237 English, *Just Watch Me*, 509.

238 http://www.nydailynews.com/news/politics/pierre-trudeau-important-message-donald-trump-1981-article-1.2971483

239 McLuhan and Fiore, *War and Peace*, 10.

240 Cook, *Teeth of Time*, 32.

Meeting of the Canadian Press, Trudeau argued: "Canada has often been called a mosaic, but I prefer the image of a tapestry, with its many threads and colours, its beautiful shapes, its intricate subtlety. If you go behind a tapestry, all you see is a mass of complicated knots. We have tied ourselves in knots, you might say. Too many Canadians only look at the tapestry of Canada that way. But if they would see it as others do, they would see what a beautiful, harmonious thing it really is."[241]

241 http://canadianart.ca/features/ken-lum-canadian-culture

More

The following are suggested as additions to the works mentioned throughout this book. For a fuller bibliography, more detailed source information and the original typos and spelling mistakes that have been corrected for this book, the reader can consult my doctoral dissertation at https://doi.org/doi:10.7282/T3BK1G98.

Anderson, Benedict. *Imagined Communities: Reflections on the Origin and Spread of Nationalism*. London: Verso, 1991.

Appadurai, Arjun. *Fear of Small Numbers: An Essay on the Geography of Anger*. Durham, NC: Duke University Press, 2006.

Berland, Jody. *North of Empire: Essays on the Cultural Technologies of Space*. Durham, NC: Duke University Press, 2009.

Bosniak, Linda. *The Citizen and the Alien: Dilemmas of Contemporary Membership*. Princeton, NJ: Princeton University Press, 2006.

Carey, James W. *Communication as Culture: Essays on Media and Society*. Boston: Unwin Hyman, 1989.

English, John, Richard Gwyn and P. Whitney Lackenbauer, eds. *The Hidden Pierre Elliott Trudeau: The Faith behind the Politics*. Toronto: Novalis, 2004.

Ferguson, Yale H. and Richard W. Mansbach. *Polities: Authority, Identities and Change*. Columbia: University of South Carolina Press, 1996.

Fischer, David Hackett. *Champlain's Dream*. New York: Simon & Schuster, 2008.

McLuhan, Marshall and Bruce R. Powers. *The Global Village: Transformations in World Life and Media in the 21st Century.* New York: Oxford University Press, 1968.

McLuhan, Stephanie and Sandy Pearl (producers). *Marshall McLuhan Speaks Special Collection.* 2015. http://www.marshallmcluhan-speaks.com.

Meyrowitz, Joshua. *No Sense of Place: The Impact of Electronic Media on Social Behavior.* New York: Oxford University Press, 1985.

New, W.H. *Borderlands: How We Talk about Canada.* Vancouver: UBC Press, 1998.

Pieterse, Jan Nederveen. *Globalization and Culture: Global Mélange* (2nd ed.). Lanham, MD: Rowman & Littlefield, 2009.

Postman, Neil. *Amusing Ourselves to Death: Public Discourse in the Age of Show Business.* New York: Penguin, 2005. Twentieth anniversary edition, with an introduction by Andrew Postman.

Powe, B.W. *Mystic Trudeau: The Fire and the Rose.* Toronto: Thomas Allen, 2007.

Strate, Lance. *Media Ecology: An Approach to Understanding the Human Condition.* New York: Peter Lang, 2017.

Trudeau, Pierre Elliott. *Against the Current: Selected Writings 1939–1996.* Edited by Gérard Pelletier. Toronto: McClelland & Stewart, 1996.

Tsing, Anna Lowenhaupt. *Friction: An Ethnography of Global Connection.* Princeton: Princeton University Press, 2005.

Acknowledgements

My late father, Ernie Kahn, taught me that a person can learn something from anyone. I would not be who I am without two particular groups of public servants, who cared about and nurtured me from a young age: the staff of the public library in Oshawa, Ontario, where I was born, and my teachers in Oshawa's public school system. My discovery of Trudeau and McLuhan while in high school was partly Zeitgeist and partly the doing of two beloved teachers who were never far from mind as I worked on this book: Murray Leslie and the late R. David McKinley.

I want to thank the official gatekeepers of the Trudeau and McLuhan papers – Marc Lalonde, Thomas Axworthy and Michael McLuhan – for permitting my access to the correspondence at Library and Archives Canada (LAC) in Ottawa. My thanks also to the LAC staff, especially archivists Catherine Butler, Robert Fisher and Genevieve Couture, for their expertise and patience over the past eight years.

Heartfelt thanks to my professors at Rutgers University in Newark, New Jersey – especially Alexander L. Hinton, Yale Ferguson and Robert W. Snyder – for their wisdom and patience, and to the directors and administrative staff of Rutgers' Division of Global Affairs.

For their advice and time, special gratitude to Professors John English at the University of Toronto and Lance Strate at Fordham University in New York; Philip Marchand; Teri McLuhan, Stephanie McLuhan-Ortved and the late Eric McLuhan. I am indebted to the staff at Novalis, especially Anne Louise Mahoney, Simon Appolloni and Glen Argan, for their expert guidance, and publisher Joseph Sinasac for his immediate and ongoing enthusiasm and support.

My father also taught me to eavesdrop. Had I not used this skill at the McLuhan centenary conference in Toronto in 2011, I would never have heard B.W. Powe mention the existence of the Trudeau-McLuhan letters. I am very grateful for B.W.'s continued unconditional help and warmth. Through B.W., I met Paolo Granata of St. Michael's College in the University of Toronto, whom I thank deeply for his thoughtful, creative foreword to this book.

I send thanks without limits to friends and family in my own global village who pushed but smiled to bring me to this moment, especially Karen Chisvin, Marianne Cobb, Ron Dressler, James Estes, Lupita Galdamez, Ellen Nesson, Jonathan Shiff, Bill Siksay, Debi Sproule and Cyrel Troster, and my sons-in-law David Freidenreich, for his advice, and Paul Pelavin, for his questions.

Love without borders to my mother, Carol Kahn; my husband, Lawrence Troster; our fiery daughters, Rachel Kahn-Troster and Sara Kahn-Troster, in whose thrall I remain; and the young ensorcellers – Liora, Aliza, Naomi and Jacob – who give me more sheer fun than I'd ever imagined for myself.

Index